EGYPT
THE AMARNA PERIOD AND THE END OF THE EIGHTEENTH DYNASTY

BY

CYRIL ALDRED

*Keeper of the Department of
Art and Archaeology
in the Royal Scottish Museum, Edinburgh*

VOLUME II, CHAPTER XIX

CAMBRIDGE
AT THE UNIVERSITY PRESS
1971

Published by the Syndics of the Cambridge University Press
Bentley House, 200 Euston Road, London NW1 2DB
American Branch: 32 East 57th Street, New York, N.Y.10022

© Cambridge University Press 1971

Library of Congress Catalogue Card Number: 73-152627

ISBN: 0 521 08210 2

Printed in Great Britain
at the University Printing House, Cambridge
(Brooke Crutchley, University Printer)

CHAPTER XIX

EGYPT: THE AMARNA PERIOD AND THE END OF THE EIGHTEENTH DYNASTY

I. THE PROBLEM OF A CO-REGENCY BETWEEN AMENOPHIS III AND AKHENATEN

Letters from Tushratta of Mitanni and Shuppiluliumash of Hatti[1] show that on the death of Amenophis III his eldest surviving son, Neferkheperure Amenhotpe (Amenophis IV), who later in his reign took the name of Akhenaten, was accepted by these foreign princes as the new pharaoh. The problem remains whether he had been recognized by the Egyptians as the co-regent of his father for some time previously. The matter has been much discussed in recent years, one body of opinion maintaining the orthodox view that Amenophis IV acceded only after the death of his father and ruled for his full term of seventeen years alone, the other interpreting ambiguous evidence, much of it recently uncovered, as revealing that the son had ruled with his father for a decade or more. No side has produced conclusive proof to convince the other, and a final decision will have to await the emergence of further evidence, perhaps in the field of comparative chronology.

The scheme of chronology adopted in this History admits of no overlap in the reigns of Amenophis III and his son;[2] a co-regency, however, must allow for a joint rule lasting some eleven years.[3] The independence of the two courts and their officials will permit these alternative interpretations, but adjustments would have to be made in the case of certain events which are treated here as occurring consecutively, whereas they may have been coeval. Thus it should be borne in mind that tendencies in art and religion, for instance, which appear in the reign of Amenophis III and are described as anticipating the innovations of Akhenaten, may in fact be contemporary with them.

---

[1] E.A. 27, E.A. 41.
[2] *C.A.H.* II², ch. ix, pt. 1, pp. 6 n. 8, 12 n. 7, 12 n. 10. See also §1, 1–21.
[3] §1, 4, 110; §1, 5, 29; §1, 10, 37.

4 THE END OF THE EIGHTEENTH DYNASTY

II. THE CHARACTER OF THE AMARNA 'REVOLUTION'

The new king was a pharaoh whose monuments have won for him, among modern scholars, the reputation of being the most remarkable king to have occupied the throne in the history of Egypt. Wide claims have been made for him as a thinker, religious reformer, artistic innovator, revolutionary and individualist.[1] It seems probable, however, that such opinions, based upon inadequate evidence, have led to many ill-founded conclusions about his originality and personal qualities. Few would now maintain that his outlook was any more international than that of other pharaohs whose sandals traditionally trod upon captive figures of the Nine Nations,[2] and who claimed to rule as gods over all that the sun encircled.

Akhenaten has also been credited with modern pacifist principles in his conduct of foreign policy that are difficult to reconcile with the testimony from damaged temple reliefs in which he appears as the conquering king smiting the age-old foes of Egypt.[3] Other scholars have seen him as a social revolutionary who chose his high officials and entourage, not from the old scribal families, but from new men of humble origins, free from hereditary traditions and orthodox habits of thought.[4] In the absence of a system of universal education in Egypt, however, it is doubtful whether the king could have found any trained personnel outside the small hereditary scribal caste who were capable of dealing with the essential paper-work by which the Egyptian bureaucratic machine functioned. Some at least of his high officials were clearly the sons of men who had held like offices during his father's reign, and it is to be suspected that many more affiliations lurk under non-committal names and titles.[5] It was a polite convention during the dynasty that such courtiers should occasionally refer to their king as having advanced them from humble origins. Thus Yuya, who was influential enough to arrange for his infant daughter to be married to Amenophis III when that king was a mere boy, refers to himself as one whom 'the pharaoh promoted and made great'.[6] Such protestations of lowli-

---

[1] G, 2, 356, 292; §II, 13, 207; §VIII, 14, 126–7.
[2] §I, 20, pl. 107B; §IV, 5, vol. I, 119; §VIII, 14, pl. XI.
[3] §II, 5, fig. 19; §VIII, 11, 47, nos. 50–51a.
[4] G, 6, 223–4; G, 8, 297–8; §II, 13, 207; §VI, 5, 539.
[5] §I, 4, 103–4; §VI, 1, 34.
[6] §II, 6, xv–xvi.

ness, like many official pronouncements in ancient Egypt, need not be taken at their face value.

The most striking of Akhenaten's innovations, and one that has gained for him the most attention in modern times, is a style of art which he instigated and which indeed seems revolutionary in its more bizarre forms, but which on closer examination is seen to be a mere distortion of the traditional manner of representing the royal family. The naturalism or realism that has been claimed for it[1] had already appeared in his father's reign.[2] Its true novelty is rather more subtle and lies in an iconography which was new and was created by artists having a non-traditional conception of spatial relationships.[3]

In only one aspect of his religious thinking is Akhenaten seen to be original—in his insistence on a true monotheism, as distinct from the henotheism of the sun-cult, which he embraced with such fervour as to arouse the strong suspicion that he was a religious fanatic. It is significant that the first great event of his reign should be a decree marshalling all the resources of the land for building temples to his god whom he identified by a didactic name which was his profession of faith—Re-Harakhte who rejoices on the horizon in his aspect of the light which is in the Aten (or Sun-disk).[4] This deity first appeared in the traditional iconic form of Re-Harakhte as a falcon-headed god, but was soon symbolized by the elaborated glyph for sunlight, a disk having a dozen or more rays emanating from it ending in hands, some of which hold the sign of life to the nostrils of the king and queen, but to no one else.[5] At the same time the enhanced divinity of the pharaoh, 'the beautiful child of the Aten',[6] is emphasized by the appointment of his own ritual priest or prophet, by the protestation or abasement of his followers when they are in his presence, and by the fact that prayers can be addressed to the god only through him as intermediary. Figures of the king and his family are substituted for Re-Harakhte at the entrance to the tombs of his officials, as indeed they replace representations of the owners themselves in all the principal scenes.[7] The old gods of burial were banished and Akhenaten's favourites prayed that in

---

[1] *E.g.* §II, 13, 214, 218–19; §III, 37, 33; §VIII, 21, 28.
[2] G, 7, fig. 142; §I, 20, 154, 180 (cf. Cairo Museum No. 33900).
[3] §VIII, 21, 11, 15. See below, sect. VIII.
[4] §III, 6, 209; §III, 24, 176.
[5] §II, 1, 24–5.
[6] G, 6, 228; §II, 13, 223–4; §IV, 17, 28; §IV, 20, 16; §VIII, 19, 91 ff.
[7] §II, 12, 84–5, 89; §III, 14, 35.

death they might rest eternally near him and behold him daily, for he was now the patron of the dead as well as of the living.[1]

In this respect, so far from being revolutionary, Akhenaten was reverting to beliefs current in the Old Kingdom when the dead in their mastaba-tombs were clustered around the pyramids of the sun-kings whom they had served in life. There is a distinct antiquarianism in this return to an earlier and more exalted status for the pharaoh which was already a feature of the preceding reign when the records of the past had been diligently searched in an endeavour to find the tomb of Osiris at Abydos and also to revive the proper ritual for the king's first jubilee.[2] It is perhaps significant in this context that a fragment of a predynastic or early archaic slate palette should survive, reworked on its reverse in the reign of Amenophis III with the name of his chief queen.[3]

This increase in the power and glory of the kingship was the inevitable political concomitant of Akhenaten's religious ideas. Such absolutism might have been effective if the king had busied himself with the *minutiae* of government, but it would seem that, absorbed as he must have been in his religious schemes, he left most of the vastly increased business of state to be carried on by his officials.[4] The introduction of monotheism into Egypt necessarily wrought changes in local affairs. The economy of Egypt was almost wholly dependent upon the utilization of land, and this was cultivated on behalf not only of the Crown and various corporate bodies, such as the royal harims, but also of the great temples of Thebes, Memphis and Heliopolis, and the local temples as well.[5] Even such a modest foundation as that of Khnum at Elephantine enjoyed income from estates which it owned as far afield as the other extremity of the country,[6] and although our information refers to conditions during the twelfth century B.C. there is no reason to believe that they differed essentially in the Eighteenth Dynasty. The dispersal of local priesthoods or the closing of the temples would have had the effect of transferring all their domains to the ownership of the pharaoh,[7] doubtless to the advantage of his deity, the Aten.

The administration of this great accession of property evidently ceased to be in the hands of the many local officials, particularly

---

[1] §II, 13, 223–4; §III, 13, Pt. I, 46.
[2] §II, 8, 462, ll. 9–10 of inscription; §II, 11, 17.
[3] Brooklyn Mus. No. 66. 175; §II, 3, 1–4.
[4] §II, 7, 156–7.   [5] §II, 9, 9–25.
[6] §II, 10, 61.
[7] *Ibid.* 23; §II, 9, 165–7, 189.

for fiscal purposes, and became the responsibility of the king's high officers of state, who may well have called upon the army as the only source of manpower able to enforce the payment of taxation. Without proper supervision the inevitable malpractices would have obtained a firm hold. Over-centralized government was doubtless to blame for the corruption, arbitrary exactions and mismanagement which Horemheb later had to suppress with a heavy hand in restoring the traditional form of government.[1]

The rapid building of the new capital city at El-Amarna and temples to the new god in every major centre must have drained the land of its labour and economic resources, and the lavish offerings to the Aten that were such a feature of the worship in the Great Temple at El-Amarna,[2] and probably elsewhere also, could only have been made at the expense of other cults. The fiscal system of Egypt had developed over the centuries and, by adjusting the claims of small local shrines, the larger temples and the departments of the Palace, had produced a system that operated without intolerable exploitation. But it must now have been overturned by new arrangements that poured the nation's resources into the coffers of the king and his god. It was doubtless the chaos caused by the economic consequences of Akhenaten's religious reforms that brought about a complete reversal to the old order as soon as he was dead. The recollection of the misery of such times was strong enough to bring upon him the odium of later generations.

III. THE REIGN OF AKHENATEN

The first important record of the new reign to have survived is a stela hewn on the east bank of the Nile at Gebel es-Silsila showing the (erased) figure of Amenophis IV wearing the Upper Egyptian crown and offering to Amon-Re.[3] The damaged text speaks of the opening of a quarry in the vicinity for extracting stone for the erection of a great benben sanctuary at Karnak for 'Re-Harakhte (who rejoices on the horizon) in his aspect of the sunlight which is in the Disk (Aten)'. For this purpose the king ordered that a muster should be made of all workmen from one end of the country to the other and that the high court officials should be put in charge of the work of cutting and transporting the stone. The quarry was evidently opened in a different place from the region

---

[1] §II, 7, 157; G, 6, 244–5; §v, 12, 311–18.
[2] §I, 18, 15, pls. VI*a*, VI*b*.
[3] G, 11, v, 220; §III, 30, 261 ff.; §VIII, 40, fig. 1.

whence came the large blocks of fine sandstone used for the great temple of Luxor, which was left unfinished on the death of Amenophis III.[1] The small size of the new blocks was probably determined less by the shallow depth of the strata from which they were prised than by the ease with which they could be handled by a large, unskilled labour force.

The impressment of workers by *corvée* shows the importance that the new king placed upon the swift fulfilment of his plans. The remains of dismantled temples to the Aten recovered from the interior of several pylons and other parts of the main temple at Karnak betray distinct signs of the haste with which they were built, particularly in the often careless and summary cutting of the reliefs in the somewhat coarse granular stone.[2] The fact that the stela at Gebel es-Silsila does not bear a date doubtless points to its being carved in the very first months of the reign. Included in the king's titulary is the designation 'First Prophet of Re-Harakhte', but, since the pharaoh was *ex officio* the chief priest of every god in the land, the special emphasis given to the sacerdotal office here probably means that he had elected to celebrate the daily ritual in the temples of the Aten and in no other.

A series of temples was built at Karnak, mostly in sandstone, but, until their dismantled parts have been studied and published in detail, it is idle to speculate on the size and nature of these edifices. While they were doubtless built in a remarkably short time, their decoration must have taken much longer to complete; it seems to reflect the changes in dogma that occurred during the years when they were being carved.[3] A temple to the Aten apparently existed at Karnak in the time of Amenophis III, if not earlier, to judge from blocks, much greater in size than those used in Akhenaten's constructions, which have been found in the core of the Tenth Pylon.[4]

Early in the reign, perhaps by the second year,[5] the Aten ceased to appear in the traditional therioanthropic form of Re-Harakhte and was represented by the symbol of the rayed disk. At the same time its didactic name was enclosed in cartouches and it acquired a titulary like a pharaoh's and an epithet to indicate that it had celebrated a jubilee.[6] Coincident with this epiphany of a heavenly king is the appearance of a new style of

---

[1] *C.A.H.* II², ch. IX, pt. 2, 35.
[2] §I, 20, 178–9; §III, 16, 113–35; §III, 41, 24 ff.
[3] §III, 1, 104.
[4] §III, 38, 28–9; §VIII, 40, pl. 4; §VIII, 46, 114; §I, 20, 179, n. 18.
[5] §II, 1, 24.   [6] §III, 24, 170–2

art which has been described as 'expressionistic' and 'realistic',[1] but the most prominent feature of which is a grotesque manner of representing the royal family, particularly the king himself, as though he suffered from a malfunctioning of the pituitary system, with an overgrown jaw, receding forehead, prominent collar-bones, pendulous breasts and paunch, inflated thighs and spindle shanks.[2] Such a marked departure from the heroic and idealistic traditions of royal portraiture could only have been taken at the instigation of the king himself, and this is made clear in the inscription of his chief sculptor Bak who claims that he was 'an apprentice whom the king himself instructed'.[3]

Temples to the Aten appear to have been raised in most of the principal towns of Egypt during these early years of the reign;[4] but however vast and numerous they may have been, the Aten could only be a parvenu on sites which had belonged to gods since they had first manifested themselves during the creation of the universe. The next ambition of Amenophis IV, therefore, was to find the 'place of origin' of the Aten and to establish there a great city dedicated to him, an ambition in which he claims to have been directed by 'Father Aten' himself.

The favoured spot selected by the king under this divine guidance proved to be a natural amphitheatre about eight miles in diameter lying on the east bank of the Nile half-way between Memphis and Thebes. To this site the modern name of Tell el-Amarna has been rather loosely applied,[5] and this in turn has been used to describe the period covered by the reign of Akhenaten. The king claimed that when found it was virgin ground which belonged to no god, goddess, prince, princess nor indeed to anyone. This may well have been the case, since no definite traces of earlier occupation have been found at El-Amarna[6] and its previous neglect was probably due to the extreme scantiness of the living that could be scratched from the strip of cultivation that bordered the river. Even today the villages on the site are comparatively recent and among the poorest in Egypt. The City of the Aten had to be sustained from the cultivation on the opposite bank, and doubtless from the rest of Egypt, as its population grew steadily during the reign.

[1] §I, 20, 179; §III, 39, 57 ff.; §VIII, 21, 28.
[2] §III, 3, 305; §III, 2, 60–1; §III, 22, 29 ff.
[3] §III, 25, 86.
[4] *E.g.* G, 11, III, 220, 222, 224; IV, 61, 63, 113, 121, 168, 259; V, 129, 144, 158, 196; VII, 73, 172–4.
[5] §III, 13, Pt. I, 1; §III, 35, 2. [6] §I, 18, 4.

10 THE END OF THE EIGHTEENTH DYNASTY

In his fourth regnal year the king, accompanied by Queen Nefertiti and his retinue, paid an official visit to the chosen site and offered a great oblation to Re-Harakhte on the festal day of demarcating Akhetaten, 'the Horizon (seat) of the Aten', as the new township was called. After summoning his courtiers and high officers to him, he showed them the site and declared that it was the Aten alone who had revealed it to him. He then swore a solemn oath that he would make Akhetaten in that place and nowhere else, even though the queen and others might try to persuade him to build it elsewhere. He went on to name the various buildings that he proposed to construct there, among them a House of the Aten, a Mansion of the Aten, a House of Rejoicing for the Aten and palaces for himself and the queen.[1] It seems likely that in this respect he was erecting the counterparts of buildings that had already been raised in Thebes and elsewhere. He also stipulated that a tomb should be cut in the eastern hills for the burial of himself, the queen and the eldest daughter, Merytaten, and that, if any of them should die in another town of Egypt, he or she should be brought to Akhetaten for burial there. The burial of the Mnevis-bull, the sacred animal of the sun-cult, should be made in the eastern hills, thus indicating that Akhetaten was to replace Heliopolis as the chief centre of sun-worship. He then promised that the tombs of his high officials should also be hewn in the same hills and, since this proposal may well have caused consternation among his followers, who would have had to abandon their family burial-grounds, he was at pains to emphasize what an evil thing it would be if they were not interred near their king.[2]

All these declarations are contained in a proclamation, unfortunately imperfectly preserved, inscribed on three heavily damaged stelae hewn into the cliffs at the northern and southern extremities of the site.[3] The royal family paid another state visit to Akhetaten in Year 6 of the reign on the second anniversary of the first demarcation and set up landmarks in the form of additional great stelae on each side of the river, giving the precise dimensions of the township and defining its boundaries, which the king swore he would not go beyond.[4] This oath has been interpreted as indicating that the king shut himself up in his holy city and did not venture beyond its confines again,[5] but this is clearly a misunderstanding and the vow appears to be no more than an

---

[1] *Ibid.* 190.   [2] §VI, 5, 300, n. 7.
[3] §III, 13, Pt. v, pls. XXIX–XXXII.   [4] See Plate Vol.
[5] *E.g.* G, 3, 64; G, 8, 295; §II, 13, 215.

affirmation by the king that he would not extend the limits of the town beyond the boundaries he had stipulated, probably for taxation purposes.[1] The entire area so designated was dedicated to the Aten, together with all its produce including its human inhabitants.

During the two years that had elapsed between the early and later proclamations, much of the central part of Akhetaten had been built and from that moment its occupation by the official classes began, if we are to judge from the incidence of dated dockets inscribed on the many sherds from broken wine-jars found on the site.[2]

The official quarters in the Central City were laid out on a fairly well-planned system, the large estates of the wealthy fronting upon two or three main thoroughfares.[3] Behind them the houses of the lesser officials were built on vacant lots and the hovels of the poor, usually sharing a common courtyard, were squeezed in wherever there was space. No system of drainage is evident and rubbish was dumped in any convenient pit or midden. The city spread northwards as its population grew and was still in process of being built when it was abandoned in the next reign. The South City housed the more important officials and was distinguished by a Maru-Aten[4] or so-called pleasure-palace, gay with a lake and basins and decorated with painted pavements and coloured inlays. Here were the kiosks or 'sunshade temples' dedicated to the daily rejuvenation of the queen and some of the princesses.[5]

The Central City contained the main official buildings such as the Great Palace, which extended for over 750 metres along one side of the principal thoroughfare and ran westwards to a frontage on the river. On its eastern boundary was the Great Temple (the 'House of the Aten') set within a huge enclosure about 750 metres long by 250 metres wide and containing several structures, notably the sanctuary and the 'House of Rejoicing' leading to the 'Gem-Aten' ('Aten is found').[6] Further south rose a smaller temple (the 'Mansion of the Aten') which appears to have been similar in design to the sanctuary of the Great Temple.[7] Both buildings appear to have been elaborations of the primitive sun-temple,[8] being a series of courts, open to the sky, with the focal

---

[1] G, 2, 365; §II, 2, 233–4.   [2] §I, 18, 160.
[3] §I, 16, 35–45; §I, 20, 186–204; §III, 17, 32 ff.
[4] §III, 32, 109–24; §III, 5, 58 ff.   [5] §I, 18, 200–8.
[6] *Ibid.* 5–20.   [7] *Ibid.* 92–100.
[8] §III, 36, 233, 237–8, 240–2.

point as an altar before a stela which took the place of the benben-stone pyramidion, as in the sanctuary of Re at Abu Ghurāb.[1] The stela, however, was an icon of the king and queen worshipping the Aten and not a sacred object of worship in itself. Because the Aten was not in tangible form, the daily ritual was of the simplest kind and centred around the presentation of lavish offerings. A later feature of the worship appears to have been the erection of a dense mass of altars in a vast area lying to the south of the 'House of Rejoicing'.[2]

Between these two temples lay such official quarters as the 'King's House', with its magazines and gardens connected by a bridge over the main road to the Great Palace.[3] Also in the vicinity were the 'House for the Correspondence of Pharaoh', where the celebrated Amarna Letters were found,[4] the Office of Works and the Police Headquarters. Half a mile downstream was the North Suburb containing the less pretentious houses of the merchants and minor officials, standing cheek by jowl with the slums of the poor.[5] The chief quays of the city appear to have been situated here and received the produce brought over daily from the cultivation on the west bank and from elsewhere. Further downstream at the extremity of the site was the North City, which has not been fully excavated or published. It contained other palaces and official quarters.[6]

The temples and the offices of the Great Palace were built of limestone, apparently quarried locally, and supplemented in certain parts with blocks of alabaster, quartzite and granite. All the domestic building, however, was in mud-brick, sometimes coated with plaster and painted. The mansions of the wealthy had stone thresholds, door-jambs, lintels, column-bases and window-grilles; bathrooms were fitted with stone splash-backs and lustration slabs.[7] Columns and doors were of wood. Such domestic architecture appears to have differed little in style and methods of construction from the palace-city of Amenophis III at Western Thebes,[8] but a novel feature of the Amarna buildings was the use of inlays of coloured stones, glass and faïence, often applied in a kind of mosaic.[9]

---

[1] §III, 7, vol. I, 7–56.   [2] §I, 18, pl. VIA.   [3] *Ibid.* 86–105.
[4] *Ibid.* 113–30; §III, 35, 23–4; §VII, 5; §VII, 7.
[5] §III, 19, 1–4.
[6] §III, 34, vol. XVII, 240–3, vol. XVIII, 143–5.
[7] §III, 19, 98–100; §I, 20, 198–204; §III, 32, 37–50.
[8] *C.A.H.* II², ch. IX, pt. I, 31 n. 2.
[9] §III, 35, 10–12, 28, pl. VI; G, 8, 288–307.

THE REIGN OF AKHENATEN

Particulars of the topography and architecture of Akhetaten have been recovered by archaeological missions from Britain, France and Germany,[1] which have dug much of the site in the present century. The tombs of the officials hewn in the cliffs and foothills on the northern and southern flanks of the eastern boundary have, however, been available for study since the days of the early Egyptologists. Their sculptured walls are the main source of our knowledge of events at El-Amarna during the king's reign and of the character of the new teaching of Akhenaten.[2]

The later boundary stelae show that, by the time they were carved in Year 6, the king had changed his *nomen* to Akhenaten, while the name of Queen Nefertiti was inflated to include the epithet Neferneferuaten. The titles of the Aten were also altered to indicate that it had celebrated a further jubilee.[3] Probably all three changes took place at the same moment. The later boundary stelae bear a codicil dated to Year 8 in which it is stated that royalty was again in Akhetaten for the purpose of inspecting the boundaries on the south-eastern frontier of the city. A more explicit reference on two of them repeats the oath of the king in fixing the limits of the city and dedicating the entire region to 'Father Aten'.[4]

At some time between this date and the pharaoh's twelfth regnal year, the didactic name of the Aten was altered from its earlier form so as to remove the last vestiges of the old therioanthropic concept from the idea of the sun as a deity.[5] The falcon-symbol, which had been combined with the hieroglyph of the sun's disk to indicate Re in his aspect of Harakhte (i.e. at his rising and setting on the eastern and western horizons) was replaced by a shepherd's crook, thereby changing the name to an abstract phrase meaning 'Re, the ruler of the horizon'. This change probably coincided with other changes of a similar kind, such as the substitution of phonetic spellings for words like 'truth' and 'mother' which had formerly been determined by hieroglyphs in the shapes of the vulture (the symbol of the goddess Mut) and the figure of a squatting woman with a feather on her head (the symbol of the goddess Maet). The new form of the name of the Aten appears at the same time as changes in its epithets, suggesting that it had celebrated a third jubilee.[6] The exact date

---

[1] §III, 32; §III, 19; §I, 18; §III, 8; §III, 10.
[2] §III, 9; §III, 13.
[3] §III, 24, 172; §II, 1, 24–31.
[4] §III, 13, Pt. v, pl. xxxiii.
[5] §III, 24, 174–6; §III, 6, 208–9.
[6] §II, 1, 30–1.

when this development occurred is not known with certainty, but there appears to be no reason to dispute the conjecture that it was in Year 9.[1]

The later form of the name of the Aten appears in the reliefs of private tombs in the northern group at Amarna, which were among the last in the series to be hewn. Two scenes in these tombs give differing versions of the presentation of gifts to the pharaoh and are dated by the text to his twelfth regnal year.[2] The representations show the king and queen being carried in their state palanquins to their thrones set up under a great baldachin at Akhetaten. With their six daughters beside them they receive gifts presented by delegates who, according to the accompanying text, came from 'Syria and Kush (the North and the South), the East and the West, and from the Islands in the Mediterranean, all countries being united for the occasion so that they might receive the king's blessing'. Representations of such ceremonies with similar texts are common in tombs of the Eighteenth Dynasty, and it has been argued that they record an event which took place on the occasion either of the king's accession to the throne or of his jubilee, and not the reception of annual tribute or plunder from successful wars, as has generally been supposed.[3] If this be so, the ceremony of Year 12 at Akhetaten must have marked either Akhenaten's accession to sole rulership or his jubilee. The alternative explanation, that Akhenaten arranged a great parade of tribute from his vassals in order to impress his followers at Akhetaten with the power and influence that he exerted abroad,[4] is difficult to reconcile with the apparent collapse of the Egyptian 'empire' in Asia during his reign.[5]

In about the same year the Queen-Mother Tiy either paid a state visit to Akhetaten with her young daughter Baketaten or took up residence there. Evidence of the visit is provided by pottery jar-dockets found at El-Amarna which mention her house and that of Baketaten.[6] Moreover her steward, Huya, was granted a tomb in the northern group, one of the last to be hewn at El-Amarna.[7] Representations in its chapel show Tiy being given a sunshade temple at Akhetaten by her son, who also furnished her with new burial equipment, evidently intending that, like her courtiers, she should be buried near him.[8] A frag-

---

[1] §III, 40, 116; §I, 18, 153. [2] §III, 13, Pt. III, pl. XIII; Pt. II, pl. XXIX.
[3] §VII, 3, 105–16. [4] §I, 16, 20–1; §III, 13, Pt. II, 43.
[5] §I, 16, 22–7; G, 2, 389. See, however, below, sect. VII.
[6] §I, 18, 164, nos. 4, 14, 200(d), (ii), (iii). [7] §III, 13, Pt. III, pl. VIII.
[8] §IV, 11, pls. XXVII–XXIX, XXXI, XXXII.

ment of a red granite sarcophagus inscribed with her name and with the praenomen of Amenophis III has been found in the Royal Tomb at El-Amarna.[1]

This tomb, in a wādi among the eastern hills at El-Amarna, was prepared as a family sepulchre in accordance with promises on the early boundary stelae. Some reliefs in the subsidiary rooms show the king and queen mourning over the bier of their second daughter, Meketaten, who died some time after the ceremony of Year 12. The presence of a nursemaid holding a baby in these scenes of poignant grief has provoked the suggestion that the princess died in childbirth,[2] which, if true, appears to indicate that the reliefs could hardly have been carved before Year 14 at the earliest. It was soon after this event that Queen Nefertiti too disappeared from the scene, her place being taken by the eldest of her six daughters, Merytaten. This change in her fortunes has been attributed to her fall from the king's favour. The evidence is largely contained in reliefs from the *maru*-temple in the southern part of the city, where a 'sunshade' dedicated to her originally has had its inscriptions and reliefs re-cut to refer to Merytaten.[3] It seems much more probable, however, that this usurpation followed on the death of Nefertiti soon after Year 14, when her sunshade was adapted to serve the needs of her eldest daughter. If she had been disgraced, much more evidence would have been forthcoming in the wholesale excision or alteration of her name and figure in the many representations of her that have survived.[4] The archaeologists who re-excavated the royal tomb in 1931 found evidence that led them to believe that the main chamber had been prepared for her burial.[5]

The place of the queen was taken for a time by her daughters, first by Merytaten and then by the latter's eldest surviving sister Ankhesenpaaten.[6] These two princesses must have played influential rôles at the court of Akhenaten in the last four years of his reign, the elder being mentioned under a hypocoristicon by foreign correspondents in some of the Amarna Letters.[7]

A notorious incident of the reign, and one that has left its mark on not a few of the standing monuments of Egypt, is the

---

[1] *Cf.* §IV, 16, 102, n. 2.
[2] §III, 9, 21, pls. VII–IX; §VIII, 14, 153; §VI, 7, 208; §III, 31, 229; For other views, see §III, 40, 116; §IV, 28, 174, n. 44.
[3] §III, 32, 154–6; §I, 5, 56–7.   [4] §II, 2, 242.
[5] G, 15, 88–9.
[6] §VII, 1, 191–3; §III, 11, 104–8; §VII, 4, 12.
[7] E.A. 10, 44; E.A. 11, rev. 26; E.A. 155, *passim*.

iconoclastic fury which the king unleashed against other cults, particularly that of the influential Amun of Thebes. His agents were active throughout the land in destroying effigies of the gods and excising their names from objects great and small. Even the cartouche of his father, which bore the hated name of Amun in its composition, did not escape the hammers of these zealots. Some at least of the extensive damage which they wrought was not repaired until the reign of Ramesses II. The precise point in the reign of Akhenaten when this campaign of persecution was instigated is difficult to place. The king's name is still given in its Amenophis form in a letter from Ghurāb dated to Year 5,[1] but on the boundary stelae of Year 6 it has changed to Akhenaten. It has been supposed, therefore, that the excisions were made about the time of the *hijrah* to Akhetaten, and later references to Amun in the reign must represent a compromise in the king's views and a partial recognition of the old proscribed cults.[2] But there is evidence that the iconoclasm may belong to the very last years of his reign.

Among the jewellery found in the vicinity of the royal tomb in 1883 and presumed to have belonged to one of the royal women who was buried there after Year 14 is a finger-ring, bearing on its bezel an inscription 'Mut, Lady of Heaven', which shows no signs of any attempt at alteration or obliteration.[3] Since such small items as scarabs often had the name of Amun excised during this period,[4] it is surprising to find that a finger-ring worn by royalty late in the reign could preserve the name of the equally ostracized Mut.

Another piece of evidence is afforded by the shrine made by Akhenaten for Queen Tiy, which bore the names of the Aten in their late form showing that it was made after Year 9 and most probably after Year 12. The words for 'truth' and 'mother' appear in its inscriptions in those phonetic forms which came into use as Akhenaten's ideas of godhead developed along more abstract and monotheistic lines. Yet it seems that when it was first carved the *nomen* of her husband had appeared on it with the Amun element intact.[5] It had subsequently been excised by the iconoclasts and the praenomen substituted in red paint. This evidence, if reliable, would support the theory that the campaign of excision and suppression took place in the last years of Akhenaten's life.

---

[1] §III, 21, 343–5.
[2] *E.g.* §I, 16, 28.
[3] §II, 2, 3, 156, pl. XII; §IV, 3, 45.
[4] §I, 18, pl. LXXVII, 6.
[5] §IV, 11, 14; §IV, 31.

THE REIGN OF AKHENATEN

The latest known date of the reign is Year 17 contained in dockets on jars found at El-Amarna, and this would appear to indicate that he died before the grape-harvest in his 18th regnal year.[1]

IV. THE IMMEDIATE SUCCESSORS OF AKHENATEN

Who the immediate successor of Akhenaten was presents a problem. In the tomb of Meryre, the Chief Steward of Nefertiti at El-Amarna, there appears a scene sketched in ink on a wall of the main hall showing the owner being rewarded for his services by a king and his queen whose names in cartouches are given as Smenkhkare and Merytaten.[2] Since the same chamber also has an elaborate relief of Meryre being rewarded by Akhenaten and Nefertiti, the presumption is that Smenkhkare succeeded Akhenaten and married his eldest daughter, by which act he strengthened any claim he may have had to the throne. Meryre continued in office as steward under the new queen, but not sufficiently long to finish the decoration of his El-Amarna tomb.

A date in Year 3 of Ankhkheperure Smenkhkare is known from a graffito scribbled in a tomb at Thebes, which also mentions his funerary temple as being in the estate of Amun, indicating that by that date at least the site of the royal tomb had reverted to the necropolis at Thebes.[3] Merytaten certainly played an important rôle at El-Amarna after the death (?) of her mother and is believed to have borne a daughter, Merytaten-tasherit, while still a princess.[4] Since Akhenaten appears to have advanced the next of his surviving daughters, Ankhesenpaaten, to her sister's position of favour before his death,[5] the evidence suggests that Smenkhkare was made co-regent and married to Merytaten before the end of the reign of Akhenaten.[6] Monuments have survived which reinforce this view. An unfinished stela from El-Amarna shows two kings seated on thrones side by side in affectionate intimacy, and another represents a young king pouring wine into an elder king's cup, much as Nefertiti was earlier shown performing that office for her husband.[7] Although the cartouches on

---

[1] §III, 18, 108–9.   [2] §III, 13, Pt. II, pl. XLI, cf. pl. XXXIII.
[3] §IV, 18, 10–11.
[4] See G. Roeder, *Amarna-Reliefs aus Hermopolis*, Hildesheim, 1969, p. 290.
[5] §III, 11, 104–8; §VII, 4, 12 n. 1; cf. §I, 20, 278 n. 4.
[6] §IV, 23, 3–9.
[7] *Ibid.* 7; §VIII, 40, pls. 30, 31; cf. §III, 13, Pt. II, pl. XXXII.

both unfinished stelae are not inscribed, it seems clear on stylistic grounds that Akhenaten and a younger co-regent are seen together, as also appears to be the case on a sculptor's model relief excavated at El-Amarna showing differing official portraits of the two kings side by side.[1] A fragmentary stela in London is inscribed with the names of Akhenaten, followed by those of Smenkhkare, above a scene which may have shown both kings together.[2] A box-lid found in the filling of the tomb of Tutankhamun bears the titularies and names of Akhenaten, Smenkhkare and Merytaten, suggesting that they were all ruling together.[3] Moreover, Smenkhkare incorporated into his cartouches epithets to show that he was 'beloved' of Akhenaten, and he also assumed the name of Neferneferuaten, which had been granted to Nefertiti in Akhenaten's sixth regnal year,[4] as though he had in some way filled the position formerly occupied by Akhenaten's chief queen.

The evidence is therefore strongly circumstantial that Smenkhkare was specially favoured by Akhenaten and appointed his co-regent. As such he would have dated the years of his rule from the time of his accession.[5] The question remains whether he survived his senior partner or died before him. A docket on a honey-jar from El-Amarna with Year 1 written below a partly expunged Year 17 is against the view that Smenkhkare enjoyed any independent rule, and most probably belongs to the successor of Akhenaten, who in that case must be the boy-king Tutankhaten.[6] This view is reinforced by another docket from a wine-jar, excavated from the Central City at Amarna, reading 'Year 1, wine of the house of Smenkhkare, deceased...',[7] which can only mean that, in the first regnal year of an undisclosed king, Smenkhkare was dead, although wine from his estate was still being bottled. The king in question must be the same Tutankhaten.

Very few of the monuments of Smenkhkare have survived. No representation in relief or statuary bears his indisputable name, and a recent attempt to identify his portraits among the Amarna sculptures has further complicated the problem by confusing his features with those of Nefertiti, Tiy, Amenophis III, Akhenaten and Ay.[8] The most reliable portrait of this king must be sought in

---

[1] §I, 18, 19, pl. LIX, 1; §III, 34, vol. XIX, 116; §IV, 14, 103; §II, 2, pl. 68.
[2] §I, 18, 231–2.   [3] §IV, 23, 5 (Carter Cat. No. 1 K).
[4] *Ibid.* 7.   [5] §IV, 19, 23.
[6] §I, 18, pl. XCV, No. 279.
[7] *Ibid.* 164, no. 8, pl. LXXVI, 35; §IV, 27, 55, D, III, 4.
[8] *Ibid. passim.*

IMMEDIATE SUCCESSORS OF AKHENATEN

the canopic coffinettes of Tutankhamun, which were originally made for Smenkhkare since they were inscribed with his name, still visible under the cartouches of the later king on the interior surfaces of their gold shells.[1] In adapting them for his successor, it is to be presumed that a minimum of alteration was made, and the portait mask on each coffinette was left untouched. Some items at least of his burial furniture were not used for his interment and appear to have been adapted for his successor, Tutankhamun.[2]

This latter king was little more than nine years old at his accession.[3] Nevertheless he was married, as custom required, to the heiress Ankhesenpaaten, the third daughter of Nefertiti and presumably the eldest surviving princess. For a time at least the pair appear to have resided in a palace in the northern quarter at El-Amarna,[4] but a decision was soon taken to abandon Akhetaten as a Residence and to make the palace quarters at Memphis, which had still been used in the previous reign, their main seat of government.[5] They evidently also refurbished the old palace of Amenophis III at Medīnet Habu for use whenever their presence was required at Thebes.[6] The artificial town of Akhetaten with its inflated population of officials, craftsmen, priests and workers and its essential garrison could not be sustained from the local resources alone, and when the Court was moved elsewhere it was inevitable that Akhetaten would no longer be able to support itself, but would dwindle to the status of a mere village. In fact, the evidence uncovered by the spade suggests that the entire area had been deserted by Ramesside times in favour of Hermopolis across the river.

The reign of Nebkheperure Tutankhaten (Tutankhamun) was comparatively short. His ninth regnal year is inscribed on two wine-jars from his tomb, and in addition four other dockets bear

---

[1] §I, 7, 137, pl. XXIII; §IV, 17, 39; §VIII, 20, pl. 46; §IV, 5, vol. III, pl. LIV; §VIII, 14, pl. XXXIV. See Plate Vol.

[2] §IV, 5, vol. II, 84–5; §I, 7, 136, 138; §IV, 29, 642 ff.; see also p. 24, n. 2.

[3] This deduction is based on the estimated length of his reign and his age at death, as revealed by his mummy. See §IV, 5, vol. II, 158–60.

[4] §III, 34, vol. XVII, 243; §I, 16, 29.

[5] G, 8, 173–6; §IV, 2, 12 n. 25; §II, 2, pls. 8, 9; §IV, 23, 8; §VI, 5, 538–9. It should be noted that this decision appears to have been taken very early in the reign. Pendlebury found houses in the northern suburbs in process of building at the time of their abandonment with little or no evidence of stonework inscribed after Akhenaten. The ring-bezels of post-Akhenaten date were inscribed for Tutankh*amun* (§III, 19, 3, 71). *Cf.* G, 6, 236.

[6] §I, 10, 177, 242.

a Year 9 which is almost certainly his.[1] Another wine-jar, dated to Year 10, also probably refers to his reign and suggests that he ruled for a full nine years.[2] Despite the finding of his burial, however, with its great wealth of golden treasure virtually intact,[3] the monuments of his reign which yield historical data are regrettably few. The most important of them is the so-called Restoration Stela, found near the Third Pylon of the temple of Amun at Karnak, which had been usurped by Horemheb.[4] It is exceptional in Egyptian annals for its confession of past sins and the frank statement of the situation that faced the young king at his accession, with the temples from one end of the country to the other fallen into neglect and the land in a state of confusion through the indifference of the offended gods. Foreign ventures met with no success and the prayers of suppliants went unanswered. The stela goes on to relate the measures which the king was taking to restore confidence in the nation and to propitiate the gods. These included the fashioning of new statues and sanctuaries of the chief deities in gold and precious stones, the repairing of their neglected shrines, the re-establishment of their daily services and offerings, and the restoration of their sequestered treasure and revenues. New priesthoods were created to re-establish the lapsed rituals, and to these were nominated the sons and daughters of notables who commanded the respect of the local populace. Most of the temple serfs and musicians were appointed from the palace staff and their upkeep was made a charge on the king's revenues. In this we may perceive a complete reversal of the policy which had been pursued by Akhenaten, whereby the local temple revenues had doubtless been diverted into the treasury of the Aten and the pharaoh.

Since the king was still a minor when these decrees were promulgated, it is clear that they were made at the suggestion of his advisers, the most prominent of whom was the vizier and regent Ay, who had served Akhenaten as a Master of the Horse and who must now have counselled a return to traditional policies that had worked well in the past.[5] The reins of government were picked up from the point where they had been dropped by Amenophis III, and a start was made on completing that king's monuments as at Luxor and Sulb.[6] The worship of Amun was restored. The royal pair changed their names so as to honour the

---

[1] §IV, 6, 3, nos. 18–23. [2] *Ibid.* no. 24; §IV, 7, 39, §3.
[3] §IV, 5; §VIII, 20; §VIII, 14; §IV, 6; §IV, 29. See Plate Vol.
[4] G, 9, no. 34183; G, 13, 2025 ff.; §IV, 2, 8–15; §V, 12, 128–35, 235–7.
[5] §IV, 24, 50–2; §V, 19, 58.   [6] §IV, 15, 3–9; §I, 21, 278.

IMMEDIATE SUCCESSORS OF AKHENATEN

god of Thebes, where a tomb was begun or extended for the young king, probably in the western branch of the Valley of the Kings, near the sepulchre of Amenophis III.[1] The mortuary temple on the west bank at Thebes is known from at least one reference[2] and this was probably in the Medīnet Habu area, though its remains have not been identified. The colossal statues destined for this temple were unfinished at the time of the king's death and were usurped by his successors.[3]

The removal of the Court from Akhetaten to Memphis, accompanied by its large retinue of officials and chamberlains, would certainly have been followed by the exodus of most of the remaining professional classes with their valuables and house-fittings.[4] Some activity was still carried on in the town, largely at the faïence- and glass-works attached to the Great Palace.[5] The withdrawal of the town garrison would have invited the looting of the local cemeteries. Those who had died there must in the main have been removed to family burial-grounds in other parts of the country, since no cemeteries, apart from a few poor burials, have been found at El-Amarna.[6] No doubt the royal burials were also transferred elsewhere. In 1907 a small tomb, No. 55, was uncovered in the Valley of the Kings at Thebes, which contained a decayed mummy in an elaborate coffin of the royal type and the remains of funerary furniture, including the dismantled parts of the large gilded wooden shrine made for Queen Tiy by Akhenaten.[7] The burial had been desecrated and the names on the coffin excised before the tomb was re-sealed in antiquity. The mummy has recently been re-examined with the aid of modern techniques by medical experts whose findings leave little room for doubt that it is of Smenkhkare, who died in his twentieth year.[8] A reappraisal of the objects left in Tomb No. 55 and the circumstances in which they were found has also recently sought to show that, before desecration, this small tomb-chamber housed the burials of Queen Tiy, Akhenaten and Smenkhkare, and that it was under Tutankhamun that their remains were deposited here.[9] It would seem that from the first there was no intention of burying Akhenaten in the tomb he had designed for himself at El-Amarna. Fragments of his alabaster canopic chest, found in the royal tomb, show no signs of the staining by the sacramental oils that would

---

[1] G, 15, 89–90, 92. [2] G, 7, fig. 191. [3] §v, 15, 101–5.
[4] §iii, 19, 3. [5] §iii, 35, 44.
[6] §iii, 32, 95; §iii, 8. [7] §iv, 11.
[8] §iii, 27, 95–119.
[9] §ii, 2, 140–62; §iii, 2, 41–65; §iv, 17, 25–40; §iv, 20, 10–25; §iv, 31, 193–9.

have been poured into it if it had ever been used.¹ It is virtually certain that other burials of the royal family, including those of Nefertiti and Meketaten were also transferred to Thebes during the reign of Tutankhamun, though their heavy stone sarcophagi were left behind, to be smashed into thousands of fragments and scattered far and wide in Ramesside times. During the transfer of the burials from the royal tomb some items of personal jewellery belonging to one of the royal women were apparently stolen and hidden nearby, to be found again in 1883 by natives during their illicit operations in the royal wādi.²

Certain objects of no intrinsic value were, however, left behind at El-Amarna, notably the master-portraits, model reliefs, plastercasts and half-completed studies found during this century in the ruins of several sculptors' studios in the town.³ These works represented defunct persons, particularly members of the royal family, whose portraits were no longer being carved. In the Bureau of the Correspondence of Pharaoh, too, was a mass of cuneiform tablets, comprising despatches from the great kings and vassal princes of Asia, which had been received during the reign and filed away in the archives. These clay tablets, the famous Amarna Letters,⁴ were also not removed, though there is some evidence that they had been buried in a hole dug beneath the office floor.⁵ It is to be presumed that the Egyptian clerks did not trouble to take away these cumbersome and weighty records, since they would probably have had copies of them written in Egyptian on easily portable papyrus, according to age-old Egyptian office procedure.⁶

Tutankhamun did not live long enough to see his policy of a return to the orthodox traditions of his dynasty take full effect. He died in his nineteenth year, perhaps as the result of a wound in the region of his left ear which penetrated the skull and resulted in a cerebral haemorrhage.⁷ How this lesion was caused must remain a mystery, but the nature and seat of the wound make it more likely to be the result of an accident than the work of an assassin.

He left no children to succeed him. Two mummified human

---

¹ §III, 26, 537.   ² §II, 2, 243, pls. XII, 109; §IV, 3, 45.
³ §I, 18, 34, 80, 81; §IV, 14, 96–101, 106; §III, 8, no. 52; §VIII, 39; §VIII, 13, pls. 12–19. See Plate Vol.
⁴ *C.A.H.* II², ch. xx, sect. 1.
⁵ §I, 18, 114; §III, 35, 23–4; *cf.* §I, 5, 34, 35.
⁶ §II, 2, 203–4.
⁷ *The Times*, Science Report, 25 October 1969: *Nature*, 224 (1969), 325–6.

foetuses found in his tomb in coffins inscribed with his name are generally taken to be his children, born prematurely and subsequently buried with him.[1] It was at his death that his widow, Queen Ankhesenamun, wrote to the Hittite King Shuppiluliumash asking him to send to Egypt one of his sons, whom she would marry and so make him pharaoh. The suspicious Shuppiluliumash hesitated too long, and when at length he despatched Zennanzash the young prince was killed while making his way to Egypt.[2]

The reason for Ankhesenamun's extraordinary request can only be surmised, but it would seem that Tutankhamun was the last male in the line of descent, and with him the family of Amosis, the virtual founder of the Eighteenth Dynasty, came to an end. Whomsoever his widow married would *ipso facto* be the next pharaoh, and in this quandary it is probable that Ankhesenamun and her advisers sought the hand of powerful foreign royalty rather than that of a native commoner, in conformity with the ideas of the age regarding the divinity of kings. The death or murder of Zennanzash, however, put an end to this scheme. The new pharaoh was the Vizier Ay, who is shown in a painting on the wall of the burial chamber of Tutankhamun's tomb officiating as the dutiful successor at the last rites.[3]

Recent attempts to interpret the inscriptions on damaged architraves retrieved from the Third Pylon at Karnak as demonstrating that Ay served for a time as the co-regent of Tutankhamun have been shown to be mistaken; such a joint rule of a young king with an aged co-regent is by its very nature exceedingly improbable.[4] There is some evidence that Ay secured the throne by marrying the royal widow in the same way as was planned for Zennanzash, since a blue glass ring, formerly in the possession of a Cairo dealer and seen by Professor Newberry in 1931, had the cartouches of Ay and Ankhesenamun engraved on its bezel, suggesting the alliance of these two persons.[5] Ankhesenamun, however, disappears from the scene after the death of her husband and the consort who is represented in the Theban tomb of King Ay is that same Tey who had appeared at El-Amarna as his wife and Nefertiti's nurse.[6]

[1] §IV, 5, vol. III, 88, 167–9.   [2] *C.A.H.* II², ch. XVII, 20.
[3] §IV, 29, 647–8, 659–60, fig. 90, pl. CXVI; §I, 20, 141 A.
[4] §IV, 28, 179; V, 12, 177–8. In a recently published inscription from Hermopolis, Tutankhaten is already described as a king's son before he came to the throne. Cf. I, 15, 317 n. 1. See G. Roeder, *Amarna- Reliefs aus Hermopolis*, pl. 106 (831–VIII–c).   [5] §IV, 24, 50.
[6] §III, 13, Pt. VI, pls. XXXI, XXXVIII, XXXIX. See Plate Vol.

Ay buried Tutankhamun in the main eastern branch of the Valley of the Kings in a small tomb which does not appear to have been the one he was preparing for himself.[1] Nevertheless, the funerary furniture that was crammed into its confined space was exceptionally rich and incorporated some of the equipment prepared for Smenkhkare's burial and evidently part of Akhenaten's also.[2]

The ill-documented reign of the aged Ay, who had served Akhenaten at least twenty years earlier as Master of the Horse, must have been short. Regnal Year 4 is his highest recorded date,[3] and he probably ruled for a little longer if the entry in Josephus for *Harmais* refers to him.[4] He presumably followed the same policy of rehabilitation that he had doubtless persuaded his predecessor to adopt. He built his mortuary temple at Medīnet Habu at the southern end of the row of such structures at western Thebes and incorporated in it a palace used during religious festivities, a feature of subsequent Ramesside mortuary temples, if indeed it had not already been anticipated by Amenophis III.[5] The entire complex was, however, taken over and extended by his successor Horemheb.

Ay prepared a tomb, No. 23, for himself in the western branch of the Valley of the Kings, near that of Amenophis III,[6] but it is probable that it had originally been started for an earlier pharaoh.[7] In the sarcophagus chamber is a wall-painting which is unique for a royal tomb and shows Ay, in company with his wife Tey, spearing a hippopotamus and fowling in the marshlands.[8] The names of the royal pair and their figures, however, have been mutilated, and the red granite sarcophagus, similar in design to those of Tutankhamun and Horemheb, has been smashed to pieces.[9] A thorough clearance of the tomb might uncover evidence to show whether Ay was ever buried there: so far his mortal remains have not come to light.

[1] G, 15, 89; §IV, 28, 179.
[2] See above, p. 19, nn. 1 and 2. According to Gardiner's note *apud* Carter's Catalogue, pectoral No. 261 P(1) [*q.v.* §IV, 30, No. 43] was inscribed for Akhenaten originally.
[3] On a stela in Berlin. G, 11, v, 22.
[4] G, 16, 103.
[5] §V, 15, 75–82; §IV, 10, pls. I, IX, X, XIV.
[6] G, 11, 1², Pt. II, 550–1.
[7] G, 15, 92.
[8] §IV, 5, 246–7, pl. XXI; §I, 20, 141 B.
[9] §III, 26, 542, pl. LVI(6); §III, 38, 3–4, pl. I[6, 7]; §VIII, 40, pl. 57.

V. THE REIGN OF HOREMHEB

Ay apparently died without living male issue and was succeeded by the Great Commander of the Army, Horemheb, who had exercised supreme power as the King's Deputy under Tutankhamun during the latter's minority.[1] It would seem that Horemheb continued to enjoy high office under Ay, and the 'Weepers Relief' in Berlin, showing a funerary procession in which the figure of a King's Scribe, Heir and Commander of the Army takes precedence over all other high officials, may date to this period.[2] The Coronation Inscription on the back of a seated dyad of himself and his wife, Queen Mutnodjme, in the Turin Museum[3] recounts the steps in his early career up to his appointment as king, and gives the impression of a smooth transfer of power from his predecessors to himself. But for ambiguous references to Horus (the ruling king) and Horus of Hnes (his divine sponsor), a critical passage in the text could be interpreted to imply that Ay accompanied Horemheb to Karnak in order to induct him as co-regent, their participation in the Festival of Southern Ope being made the occasion of obtaining the recognition of the gods.[4] At least the unusual phrase in which he is referred to as 'the eldest son of Horus' suggests that he had been appointed the heir of Ay.[5] The fact that Horemheb considered himself in the proper line of descent and not as a usurper or the founder of a new dynasty is to be inferred from the formation of his praenomen with the 'kheperu-re' element, in which he followed the fashion set by nearly all the kings of the Eighteenth Dynasty and certainly by his Amarna predecessors.

The dated documents of the reign are scanty, Years 1, 3, 7 and 8 only having been preserved for certain, so that recently the view has been challenged that Horemheb enjoyed a long rule of between 25 and 30 years,[6] which follows if the date recorded in the inscription of Mes is accepted.[7] A hieratic graffito found at Medīnet Habu and mentioning a Year 27 must be regarded as too ambiguous to be admitted alone to consideration.[8] It has been argued that the absence of any date after the first eight years, which are consistently documented, is significant. The paucity of

---

[1] §v, 23, 1–5; v, 12, 45–9.
[2] §v, 21, 56–8; §v, 12, 63–4; §v, 19, 59–61; §ii, 2, pl. 78; §iii, 29, pls. 54–5. See Plate Vol.
[3] §v, 10, 13–51.
[4] *Ibid.* pl. ii, ll. 4, 12–14.
[5] *Ibid.* l. 12; §v, 12, 211 n. 198.
[6] §v, 13, 95–9; *cf.* §v, 6, 33.
[7] §v, 8, 3; §v, 12, 405–9.
[8] §v, 15, 106–8; §i, 18, 157–8; §v, 12, 354–5; §v, 13, 96.

26   THE END OF THE EIGHTEENTH DYNASTY

the monuments of Horemheb which have survived is also taken as an indication of the shortness of his reign. This is not the place to discuss those arguments, which are made largely *ex silentio*; suffice it to say that the chronology followed in his work demands a reign for Horemheb of some 27 years determined by the Mes date.

Horemheb has often been identified with the King's Scribe, Steward, Master of Works and Commander of the Troops of the King (Akhenaten), Paatenemheb, who had started to cut a tomb among the southern group at El-Amarna, but the equation cannot be proved and remains doubtful.[1] Horemheb makes his first unequivocal appearance at the beginning of the reign of Tutankhamun, and, despite the high military rank which he held, he must be classed as a staff officer rather than a field commander.[2] It may have been his organizing ability which first marked him for preferment. In the tomb which he constructed for himself at Memphis as a private person, he makes a passing reference to having accompanied his lord (doubtless the young Tutankhamun) on the battlefield in Asia,[3] which may refer to some parade of force early in the reign in the disaffected areas of Palestine.

Another early inscription on the Zinzinia fragment[4] almost certainly refers to a diplomatic mission that he undertook to secure the allegiance of the Nubian and Kushite native governors at the accession of the same boy-king, rather than to some military expedition in those regions.[5] We are also to infer from his Memphite tomb-reliefs that he acted as the mouth-piece of the king in dealings with foreign legates and Egyptian provincial governors alike.[6] On the death of Tutankhamun he appears to have continued in office under Ay, being accepted as the heir apparent and probably being created co-regent in the last years of the reign. During this period he must have played a key rôle in the rehabilitation of the country, for in the Coronation Inscription he claims to have renewed the temples from one end of the land to the other, fashioning statues of the gods and re-establishing their endowments and services, in much the same way as Tutankhamun in his Restoration Stela speaks of his work of reparation a decade or so earlier. It is perhaps significant that

[1] §v, 12, 35–6, 41; §v, 19, 60; G, 4, 350.
[2] §vi, 4, 43, 78–84; §vi, 5, 371–4, 486–7.
[3] §v, 16, 16. See below, pp. 38–9.
[4] §v, 12, 64–8; §v, 9, 3.
[5] §vii, 3, 108.
[6] §v, 9, 5, 7–8; §v, 10, pl. ii, l. 7; §v, 12, 113–14; §vi, 5, 373.

Horemheb should in his lifetime have usurped this stela of the king he had once served.¹

During his sojourn with the court at Memphis he built a tomb in the nearby necropolis decorated with fine reliefs now dispersed among several museums.² An uraeus has been added later to the brow of Horemheb in these reliefs, though no alterations to the texts and other figures appear to have been made.³ A second tomb, however, was cut for him in due course in the royal necropolis at Thebes in which he appears to have been buried, though no part of his human remains has been identified among the débris found there.⁴

As has been mentioned above, his surviving monuments are relatively few having regard to the length of time he is presumed to have ruled; but this is true for all the immediate post-Amarna kings, and the presumption is that they were so fully occupied with the re-building and re-endowment of the temples up and down the country that they had little resources of labour and treasure to expend on new constructions. In this context it is significant to note that in his nine years of rule Tutankhamun was able only to finish the companion to the granite lion of Amenophis III in the temple of Sulb, and it was left to his successor, Ay, to transport it from the quarry to the site.⁵ Nevertheless, apart from his restorations, the building enterprises of Horemheb were far from inconsiderable. He enlarged the mortuary temple of Ay for his own use, or their joint cult, until it assumed gigantic proportions,⁶ though it has now almost totally disappeared. At Karnak he seems to have planned and begun the great Hypostyle Hall of the Temple of Amun and the Second Pylon, using in their foundations and cores blocks from the Aten temples of Akhenaten in the vicinity, though it was left to his successors in the following dynasty to complete these works.⁷ He also raised other pylons, the Ninth and Tenth on the processional way to the south of the temple, and joined them by walls forming a large court enclosing on the east side the jubilee temple of Amenophis II.⁸ The towers of these great gateways were also filled with thousands of small blocks from the dismantled temples of the Aten.⁹ Both pylons were usurped by later kings and are now greatly ruined.

---

¹ §v, 12, 130.
² §v, 12, 69–125; §v, 5, 2 ff.; §viii, 11, 23–4; §v, 3, 31 ff.; §viii, 13, 27–31.
³ §v, 2, 49–50. ⁴ §v, 6; G, 15, 92–6.
⁵ §iv, 15, 9. ⁶ §v, 15, 78.
⁷ §v, 20, 7 ff.; §v, 12, 329. ⁸ G, 11, 11, 59–63; §v, 12, 331–7.
⁹ §iii, 16; §iii, 12; §iii, 41.

28 THE END OF THE EIGHTEENTH DYNASTY

Before them stood a total of six colossi in red quartzite of the king, with Queen Mutnodjme on a much smaller scale. It is probable, however, that some at least of these statues were already lying on the site, but still unfinished, from the days when Amenophis III planned the erection of the Tenth Pylon.[1] The great avenue of crio-sphinxes that connected this latter gateway to the temple of Mut also appears to be the work of Horemheb, though usurped by others.[2]

At Gebel es-Silsila he cut and decorated with fine reliefs a *speos* in the cliffs on the western bank.[3] A similar rock temple, but on a smaller scale, was hewn out of the cliffs at Gebel Adda in Nubia and dedicated to Amun and Thoth.[4] At Memphis he erected buildings in the precints of Ptah, as a damaged stela bearing a version of the Coronation Inscription proclaims, and these included a temple furnished with the usual cedar flag-poles and embellished with gold and Asiatic copper.[5] It is also certain that similar constructions were raised in Heliopolis.[6]

The tomb that the king cut at Thebes is among the largest in the Valley of the Kings and followed the fashion introduced into the design of such royal hypogea by Akhenaten at El-Amarna, being virtually a long corridor driven into the hillside and leading to the burial vault.[7] It is decorated in those parts which it was customary to embellish in the Eighteenth Dynasty, but it differs from earlier examples in having its scenes cut in relief and not painted on plaster. It also introduces for the first time in a royal tomb extracts from *The Book of Gates* which are inscribed on the walls of the pillared burial hall.[8] The decoration is almost complete except for some reliefs in the latter chamber which are in various stages of being sketched, carved and painted. It would be rash, however, to draw inferences as to the length of the king's reign from this circumstance. The paintings, for instance, in the tomb of Amenophis III, who had a long reign, are also incomplete.[9] Doubtless all kings depended upon the piety of their successors for finishing off their tombs before they were buried in them. Horemheb was unfortunate in being followed by a king who had the briefest of reigns.[10]

[1] G, 11, II, 62. It is difficult to see otherwise why the statues of Amenophis son of Hapu should have been placed here; (but cf. §v, 12, 256–7).
[2] §v, 12, 282–3.   [3] G, 11, v, 208–13; §v, 12, 359–70.
[4] G, 11, VII, 119–21.   [5] §v, 10, 30, 31.
[6] §v, 12, 289–92, 386; §G, 11, IV, 63, 70.
[7] §v, 6.
[8] G, 15, 94–5; G, 11, 1², Pt. II, p. 568.
[9] §v, 18, 116.   [10] §v, 1, 102 n. 1.

THE REIGN OF HOREMHEB

It may well have been that Horemheb did not begin to cut his Theban tomb until his later years. There is some evidence that the workmen's village at Deir el-Medīna, on the west of Thebes,[1] was only being re-established in this reign.[2] The policing of the Valley of the Kings, at all events, appears to have been negligent during his earlier years, for tomb-robbers were active in the Valley at this period and had evidently broken into several tombs including those of Tuthmosis IV and Tutankhamun.[3] It was in his Regnal Year 8 that Horemheb had to renew the burial of the former and it was probably at the same time that the violated tomb of the latter was cleared up. It seems incredible that Horemheb's tomb could have been in process of construction about 150 metres from the spot where another royal tomb was being violated, and the inference is that it had not at that time been started.

This pillaging is but one indication of a general lawlessness that seems to have prevailed since the end of the reign of Akhenaten, and suggests that the disorder referred to by Tutankhamun in his Restoration Stela had by no means been curbed. The great granite stela which Horemheb erected against the north face of the western tower of the Ninth Pylon at Karnak bears other witness to this general unrest.[4] The woefully damaged text which is usually referred to as 'The Edict of Horemheb' appears to be a selection of the ordinances which the king issued 'to seek the welfare of Egypt' by suppressing illegal acts.

It seems clear from this Edict that the central authority of the Crown had grown considerably, presumably at the expense of the religious foundations both local and national, and much of the administration had in consequence fallen into the hands of court officials, notably of the army, so removing any local checks and balances that the former system may have enjoyed. The result had been widespread corruption, the oppression of freemen by fraudulent tax-collectors, and arbitrary exactions and requisitions by an undisciplined soldiery in the name of the king. Both the tax-paying populace and the crown had been cheated by this extortion, and the enactments were designed to protect the interests of both. In his edict Horemheb quotes examples of

---

[1] *C.A.H.* II², ch. xxxv, sect. III, 21.

[2] Verbal communication by the late Prof. Jaroslav Černý.

[3] §v, 4, xxxiii–iv, figs. 7, 8; §v, 12, 393, pl. LX; §IV, 5, vol. I, 54, 93; vol. III, 85–6.

[4] §v, 12, 302–18; G, 1, III, §§45–67; §v, 17, 260–76; §v, 14, 109–36; §v, 22, 230–8.

abuses that had developed, and threatens future transgressors with savage punishments. At the same time he announces that he has appointed reliable men as supreme judges (viziers) in the two capital cities of Memphis and Thebes and has adjured them to hold themselves aloof from other men and not to accept bribes or presents from them. The district tribunals were also reorganized to consist of the headman of the region and functionaries and ritual priests of the local temples. If any member of these councils should be accused of practising injustice, he would have to answer a capital charge. On the other hand, those judges who performed their duties conscientiously were to have the honour of being rewarded periodically by the king in person.

Despite the numerous lacunae in the edict, several facts emerge from its study, such as the organization of the army into two main divisions, one serving in Upper and the other in Lower Egypt, a system which still prevailed when Herodotus visited the land some nine hundred years later and which probably dated from the beginning of the New Kingdom. Nevertheless, the plundering of the inhabitants by a rapacious army implies that a reform of its command was a necessary preliminary to Horemheb's measures to restore justice, and is already implicit in his statement in the Coronation Inscription that the priesthoods had been re-established from the 'pick of the army', presumably referring to its administrators, a rather different method of recruitment from that employed a decade earlier, when they were drawn from the families of local worthies.[1] Remarkable, also, is the return of supreme judicial power to the viziers in Memphis and Thebes, presumably in place of favourites of the king such as the High Stewards and Butlers, to whom royal authority had so often been delegated in the Eighteenth Dynasty from Hatshepsut onwards.

The success of Horemheb's reforms must have owed not a little to the tours of inspection which he claims to have made throughout the length and breadth of Egypt to ensure that his new measures were enacted with vigour, and that fresh abuses had no chance to develop. But whether he acted thus on behalf of the kings he served in his early career or only when he came to the throne is obscure, since the Coronation Inscription does not specifically mention these activities and the edict lacks its critical date.[2]

If Horemheb had any sons by his principal queen, Mutnodjme, they do not appear to have survived him and he was

[1] §v, 10, pl. II, l. 25, p. 21 n. 3j; §IV, 2, 10, l. 17.
[2] But cf. §v, 12, 307–8.

succeeded by a Ramesses whose claim to the throne is uncertain, but whose former identification with the Vizier and deputy, Pramesse, has apparently to be abandoned.¹ Ramesses, the first of that name, evidently hailed from the Delta and was regarded as founding a new dynasty, his praenomen setting a new pattern in royal nomenclature. His reign was too brief to decide whether it was he who instituted the policy which his son and grandson followed of execrating the Amarna pharaohs, destroying their monuments and suppressing their records.² He must have been of advanced years when he ascended the throne, for his son, Sethos, was then a man in the full vigour of life. A fragment of a model obelisk giving part of the titularies of Horemheb and Ramesses I suggests that the former king had associated the latter on the throne with him for some years before his death.³

VI. THE ROYAL FAMILY AT THE END OF THE EIGHTEENTH DYNASTY

It is clear that around the kings of the Fourth Dynasty, for instance, there clustered many officials who were closely related to them,⁴ but, because our documentation is far less complete for other periods, it is generally assumed that the custom of appointing viziers and other high officers of state from the circle of the royal family was abandoned in the later Old Kingdom. Thus the title 'King's Acquaintance' was not regarded then as signifying that its owner was a relation of the pharaoh.

In the Eighteenth Dynasty, however, sufficient evidence has survived to encourage the view that many of the king's entourage were related to him, either directly or by virtue of some less exalted familial bond.⁵ Apart from the junior sons and daughters who all had to be brought up to wear the purple, in case it should fall to their lot, as it so often did, by the premature demise of elder brothers and sisters,⁶ there were also collateral descendants from earlier reigns, foster-brothers whose mothers had acted as wet-nurses of the kings⁷ and high officials whose daughters had entered the royal harims⁸ or who had been honoured by the gift of a wife brought up in such an institution.⁹ In exceptional

---

¹ §v, 11, 23–9.
² §v, 12, 167; §viii, 11, 2; §iii, 2, 59; §v, 13, 96 n. 9.
³ §v, 1, 100–3.   ⁴ G, 8, 62.
⁵ §vi, 5, 254, 279–80; cf. §vi, 4, 31 n. 2, 66–71; G, 8, 268; §vi, 1, 30–1.
⁶ For deceased eldest sons see §vi, 3, 15; *C.A.H.* ii², ch. ix, pt. 1, 6, 11.
⁷ *C.A.H.* ii², ch. ix, pt. 1, 5; §vi, 4, 66–73; §1, 10, 238.
⁸ G, 5, 1, no. 127; §vi, 1, 35–6.   ⁹ §vi, 9. no. 51005 *passim*.

circumstances men who were not in the direct line of descent, such as Tuthmosis I,[1] or even commoners without evidence of royal blood in their veins, such as Ay,[2] might marry the heiress daughter of the pharaoh.

It is difficult to trace such relationships in detail because, for the most part, the officials are extremely reticent in mentioning their connexions with the royal house, but there is little doubt that such kinsmen must have formed veritable dynasties around the dynasties of the kings and queens whom they served, and the ramifications of one or two influential families can be traced to show the interdependence of the ruling caste of Egypt at this period.[3]

A notable case in point is the family of Queen Tiy, the chief wife of Amenophis III, who is usually regarded as a commoner whom the King married as the result of a 'love-match'.[4] As Amenophis III could not have been more than eight years old at his accession, it can be presumed that romantic passion played no part in this alliance and that the infant Tiy must have had influential supporters. Her father Yuya was an experienced officer of chariotry and the Master of the Horse. It is to be suspected that he was related to the Queen Mother, Mutemwiya, and was perhaps the uncle of the young king.[5] He was in any case sufficiently important and well known to have his name and that of his wife mentioned in the rescript of the infant king's accession.[6] He came from the provincial city of Akhmīm, where he and his wife held important and lucrative sacerdotal positions and in the vicinity of which Tiy acquired large estates.[7] One of his sons, Anen, held the office of Second Prophet of Amun in Thebes and Chief Seer in the temple of Re in Karnak.[8] It is also likely that Yuya had another son, Ay, who held his father's office of Master of Horse under Akhenaten and who as king built a rock-temple to Min in the family seat of Akhmīm at a time when little new constructional work was undertaken.[9]

Like his father before him, Akhenaten appears to have married a cousin as his chief wife, for Nefertiti has been identified as the daughter of Ay.[10] It was probably by virtue of this relationship,

---

[1] *C.A.H.* II², ch. IX, pt. 1, 5; §VI, 1, 30–1.
[2] *Ibid.* 35–7.
[3] *E.g.* §VI, 5, 435(4), 499(8); §VI, 1, 30.
[4] *E.g.* §VI, 5, 538.
[5] §II, 2, 40, 42, 88–9.   [6] §VI, 2, 5, pls. I–IX.
[7] §VI, 13, 23–33.   [8] §VI, 1, 32; §I, 19, 137; §I, 21, 275.   [9] §VI, 1, 33.
[10] §II, 2, 89–92; §VI, 1, 37–9; §V, 12, 171–4; §V, 1, 105–6.

if not some closer ties with the royal house, that Ay eventually ascended the throne on the extinction of the direct line.

In addition to the many foreign marriages which Amenophis III made for diplomatic reasons, he also wedded several of his daughters,[1] a practice which appears to have been followed by Akhenaten, and although these incestuous unions seem to have been as much permitted to the pharaohs as to the ancient Hebrews, for instance,[2] the custom has been dismissed as no more than a symbolic rite enabling the princesses to act as deputies of the queen in ceremonies in which she played an essential rôle, even though they were mere infants.[3] Since Akhenaten's daughters, however, are known to have had children while they were still princesses, not having their names enclosed in cartouches, it is difficult to accept these marriages as purely nominal.[4] The custom in fact may have been more general than is supposed, our documentation on the subject being a little fuller for this period than for nearly all other reigns, though it is noteworthy that Ramesses II also married some of his own daughters.[5]

Some ambiguity exists about the exact relationship of Smenkhkare and Tutankhamun to the ruling house. That they legitimized their claims to the throne by marrying the eldest surviving heiress queen is certain, but it is to be suspected that they had strong rights of their own. In the case of the latter king there is little doubt in the matter, since he was only eight or nine at his accession, and a newly published inscription from Hermopolis names him, while still uncrowned, as the son of a king 'of his loins'.[6] As he had been born at least four years before Smenkhkare came to the throne, his claims would not have been passed over, young as he was, if his predecessor too had not been the son of a king. The mortal remains of these two pharaohs have such close physical resemblances that they have long been regarded as brothers, a view that has recently been strengthened by the recognition that they belong to the same blood groups, A_2 and MN.[7]

The problem remains of the identity of the king whose sons

---

[1] §vi, 12, 36–54.

[2] *Lev.* 18, 6ff., 20, 10ff.; *Deut.* 27, 20ff.

[3] §vi, 6, 24.

[4] §iii, 11, 104–8; §vi, 8, no. 9. This relief from Hermopolis shows a king followed by Ankhesenpaaten, her name not enclosed in a cartouche, with her daughter behind her, but on a lower block not so far located.

[5] *Cf.* §iii, 31, 229.

[6] See above, p. 23, n. 4. *Cf.* §iv, 28, 178, 179.

[7] See above, p. 22, no. 7.

these brothers are. Tutankhamun states that Amenophis III is 'his father' (as distinct from 'the father of his father'),[1] but most Egyptologists refuse to accept this claim and dismiss it as merely implying that Amenophis III was his ancestor. If, on the other hand, Akhenaten was the father of these two princes, Smenkhkare must have been born at the latest soon after he had come to the throne, and more probably three years before. If this is so, their mother remains unidentified, but is unlikely to have been Nefertiti who, despite the unprecedented way in which her domestic life with the king is frankly depicted, is never shown as the proud mother of the heirs apparent. Despite, too, the intimacy in which Smenkhkare is shown with Akhenaten, calling himself 'beloved' of the older king, he never pretends to be his son, which was the closest relationship that it was possible for him to claim. While, therefore, it remains doubtful whether Akhenaten was the father of Smenkhkare and Tutankhamun, the paternity of Amenophis III can only be admitted in their case if there was a long co-regency between him and Akhenaten,[2] since Tutankhamun must have been born in Akhenaten's twelfth regnal year at the very latest.

Ay certainly gained the throne on the death of Tutankhamun, but that he married the royal widow is denied by some historians,[3] the evidence of the ring inscribed with his name and that of Ankhesenamun being considered too flimsy for admission.[4] It seems inevitable, however, that Ay would have confirmed his shaky right to the throne by the time-honoured custom of marrying the royal heiress, even though in his case she may have been his grand-daughter, since this was to have been the means by which the prince Zennanzash was to be made pharaoh. Ay, the putative father of Nefertiti, almost certainly had other children, including that Mutnodjme who at El-Amarna is described as the 'sister' of Nefertiti.[5] From the early days of Egyptology she has been identified as the woman who later married Horemheb, and as the royal heiress furnished her husband with his right to the throne. Whether Horemheb married her in his early years and by this alliance climbed to a position of influence at the court, or only espoused her on his nomination to the crown is problematic.[6] It is also doubtful whether the family of Ay succeeded in maintaining its position in the next dynasty. A faïence knob, however,

---

[1] §IV, 21, 76; §I, 21, 279.
[2] See above, sect. I.
[3] G, 6, 236; §IV, 28, 180.
[4] See above, p. 23.
[5] §VI, 1, 39, 41; §V, 12, 171–6; §V, 1, 103–6.
[6] §VI, 1, 41; §V, 12, 78, 232.

bearing his cartouche and evidently from a piece of furniture deposited as an heirloom in the tomb of Queen Nefertari-merymut may be not without significance.[1] This queen was the chief wife of Ramesses II during his early years and must have been given to him in marriage on his appointment as co-regent. She bears a name not unknown in the family of Ay, who were devoted to the worship of Mut,[2] and she may therefore have been a connecting link between the two dynasties.

VII. FOREIGN AFFAIRS

The victory of Megiddo, won by Tuthmosis III in his twenty-third regnal year over a confederation of Asiatic princelings, asserted Egyptian claims in Syria which had been challenged in the earlier years of the Eighteenth Dynasty by the vigorous and rising power of the Mitanni.[3] The successors of Tuthmosis III, however, were unable or unwilling to maintain their pretensions over vassal states in North Syria and came to an understanding with other Great Powers in the Near East to define their spheres of influence.[4] A treaty with the Khatti was arranged early in the career of Tuthmosis III[5] and was apparently still in force during the reign of Amenophis III.[6] Babylonia also had a pact of mutual assistance with Egypt and invoked it to warn the Canaanites from attacking the territory of its ally.[7]

Such treaties were cemented by marriages between the daughters of the royal houses and the pharaoh, the most documented of such alliances being the series of marriages between princesses of the Mitanni and Tuthmosis IV, Amenophis III and Akhenaten.[8] The daughters of less exalted princes, however, also entered the royal harims in Egypt and played their part in the diplomacy of the age.[9]

Within its Asiatic sphere of influence, Egypt hardly exercised any Roman *imperium*, despite some ambiguous indications of its exploitation of the region.[10] The pharaoh as the traditional vanquisher of the Nine Nations was the divine overlord whom vassals in Palestine and Syria addressed as 'my sun', 'my god', 'my

---

[1] §vi, 11, 55, 103, fig. 82.
[2] §vi, 1, 33 n. 1; §ii, 2, 88, pl. 66; §v, 10, 66–8.
[3] *C.A.H.* ii², ch. xv*a*, 15.   [4] *Ibid.* 19.
[5] *Ibid.* 11, 15, 37.   [6] E.A. 41; §vii, 4, 22 n. 1.
[7] E.A. 9; *C.A.H.* ii², ch. xviii, 7.
[8] E.A. 17, 26 ff.; E.A. 19, 17 ff.; E.A. 22, iv, 43 ff.; E.A. 24, iii, 9 ff.; E.A. 29, 16 ff.; §vi, 2, pl. xxix.
[9] E.A. 31; E.A. 31*a*; §vii, 9, 41, 47.   [10] *C.A.H.* ii², ch. xx, 9–11.

'lord' and in similar terms of subservience.[1] Apart from this spiritual leadership, however, it is doubtful whether anything like an empire existed[2] and the scenes of foreigners bearing tribute to lay before the mercy-seat of the pharaoh are capable of other interpretations than the mercantile development of the region.[3]

The many vassal states kept up interminable internecine squabbles, their main objective being to preserve their own autonomy, to extend their frontiers and power at the expense of their weaker neighbours and to enlist the military might and resources of their overlord, ostensibly to protect his interests, but actually to advance their own ambitions.[4] They therefore set up a constant clamour for help to preserve the town or state they were so loyally defending, coupled with assurances of their own honesty and fidelity and the treachery and ruthlessness of their rivals.[5]

Despite the remoteness of these quarrels from the centre of government in Egypt, it seems highly probable that the Egyptians, informed by despatches from their own commissioners and garrison commanders, had a good idea of what was afoot and took the action that seemed best to them, though modern observers of the partially revealed scene have not been slow to level charges of supineness and muddle against the Egyptian administration.[6]

The treaties between the Great Powers of the Near East, however, brought a period of comparative calm and stability to Palestine and South Syria during the reigns of Tuthmosis IV and Amenophis III, when the Egyptian garrisons in key cities such as Gaza, Beth-shan, Joppa, Sumura, Rehōb and Megiddo were able to reinforce local levies in checking the pretensions of the more turbulent dynasts and in repressing the Shasu bedawin and the Apiru freebooters who posed a constant threat to law and order.[7]

With the accession of Shuppiluliumash to the Hittite throne, however, about the second decade of the reign of Amenophis III,[8] a new actor appeared on the scene who was to remould decisively the political structure of the region during the following century. The struggle that now developed between the Khatti and the

---

[1] *Cf.* E.A. 60, 1–7; E.A. 76, 1–6; E.A. 176a, 1–6; E.A. 270, 1–8.
[2] G, 6, 230; §vii, 3, 111.   [3] *Ibid.* 105–16.
[4] *C.A.H.* ii², ch. xx, 8–9; §vii, 4, 14.   [5] §vii, 8, 60–3.
[6] G, 2, 379, 385–6; §ii, 13, 207, 230–1.
[7] *C.A.H.* ii², ch. i, 29–30; *C.A.H.* ii², ch. xx, 14–18.
[8] *Ibid.* ch. xviii, 8; §vii, 4, 39.

FOREIGN AFFAIRS

Mitanni for supremacy involved the vassal states of Egypt on her borders with these two powers and ultimately led to the wars of attrition between Egypt and the Khatti in the early Nineteenth Dynasty.[1]

The Egyptian records from the death of Amenophis III to the accession of Sethos I are too scanty and incomplete to give any coherent picture of the foreign scene as viewed through Egyptian eyes. The outlines have therefore to be sketched from the cuneiform archives found at El-Amarna and Boğazköy, and the situation prevailing when Sethos I began his Asiatic campaigns in his first regnal year.[2]

The protracted struggle between Tushratta of the Mitanni and Shuppiluliumash of the Khatti is recounted elsewhere.[3] The Egyptians had treaties with both nations and appear to have shown little inclination to intervene, a policy which has been accredited to the neglect by Akhenaten of the affairs of his 'empire' rather than to the preservation of a strict neutrality. It may have been immaterial to the Egyptians which of the two rivals had suzerainty in North Syria, since they themselves were evidently unwilling to exercise any dominion over the region. Their efforts appear to have been reserved for trying to maintain their influence in the coastal area stretching from Byblos in the south to Ugarit in the north. In this policy they found themselves dealing with the astute and turbulent princes of the Amurru, whose domains straddled the region and who found the confusion caused by the wars between the Khatti and the Mitanni congenial to their own expansionist aims.[4]

Abdi-ashirta, the first of these Amurru princes, made a show of recognizing Egyptian suzerainty on the North Syrian coast, but his intrigues eventually exhausted Egyptian patience and he was slain by a task-force of marines in the last years of Amenophis III or early in the reign of Akhenaten.[5] His equally troublesome successor, Aziru, was summoned to the Egyptian court to give an account of himself and to serve as hostage for the good behaviour of his state.[6] Though he eventually returned to the Amurru with the confidence of the pharaoh, the pressure of events left him no option but to become the faithful vassal of Shuppiluliumash.[7]

By the end of the reign of Akhenaten, Egypt had proved a broken reed in its failure to support the independent states of

---

[1] *C.A.H.* II², ch. XXIII, 12–15.
[2] G, 6, 252–5.
[3] *C.A.H.* II², ch. XVII.
[4] *Ibid.* 12–15.
[5] §VII, 4, 27–8.
[6] E.A. 161, 22 ff.; E.A. 164, 14 ff.
[7] *C.A.H.* II², ch. XVII, 14–17; §IV, 4, 17–18.

South Syria with effective military aid. Qatna, Nukhash, Qadesh and above all the Amurru passed into Hittite vassalage.[1] It is doubtless this loss of influence which is referred to in the Restoration Stela of Tutankhamun when it is admitted with rare candour that, if in the days of his predecessor an army was sent to Syria to extend the boundaries of Egypt, it met with no success.[2] It would appear, however, that some attempt was made during the reign of Tutankhamun to recover lost ground, a more aggressive policy being promised to the king's District Commissioners in an inscription in the Memphite tomb of Horemheb, where the owner is spoken of as 'the guardian of the footsteps of his lord on the battlefield on this day of smiting Asiatics'.[3] The cuneiform records reveal that the Hittites raided Amqa between the Lebanon and Antilebanon, which was a violation of Egyptian-held territory. As a riposte the Egyptian forces captured Qadesh on the Orontes and doubtless encouraged the revolt of Nukhash.[4] Their triumph was shortlived, however, for in the following year a Hittite force drove the Egyptians from Qadesh and re-entered Amqa. It was at this point that Tutankhamun died and his widow petitioned Shuppiluliumash to give her one of his sons in marriage.[5] After the murder of Zennanzash, Shuppiluluimash again attacked Amqa, defeated the Egyptian forces and brought back prisoners who carried with them a plague which spread among their captors and became endemic among the Khatti for years afterwards.[6]

Evidently the Hittites realized that by their aggression they had broken the terms of their treaty with Egypt, a pact which had been sealed by oaths to the gods, probably of both powers,[7] who were now accredited in their anger with visiting the plague upon the violators. Shuppiluliumash himself died of the disease early in the reign of Horemheb and his successor, Murshilish, undertook penances to deflect the wrath of the gods, making restitution and returning prisoners to Amqa.[8] It seems probable therefore that the frontiers of Egypt and of the Khatti were stabilized at the Lebanon throughout the reign of Horemheb and that Egyptian policy was confined to trying to exert the claims over the Amurru and Ugarit which it had exercised in the prosperous days of Amenophis III. In this it appears to have

---

[1] $C.A.H.$ II², ch. XVIII, 17–18; §IV, 4, 46.
[2] G, 13, 2025 ff.; §IV, 2, 9, l. 9.   [3] §V, 16, 16; §V, 9, 7.
[4] $C.A.H.$ II², ch. XVII, 19; §IV, 4, 47.
[5] $C.A.H.$ II², ch. XVII, 19–20.   [6] §VIII, 34, 395.
[7] $Cf.$ §VII, 6, 197.   [8] §VIII, 34, 396.

enjoyed some temporary success, but was defeated by the superior skill of Murshilish.[1]

Further south in Palestine the task of the Egyptians in maintaining their influence was simpler, since here they were not opposed by a unified great power commanding trained military forces and enjoying interior lines of communication. This area was also in a constant state of unrest caused by the rivalries and feuds of local princes, whom it was not difficult to divide and rule. In the reign of Akhenaten a more serious threat developed in Central Palestine through the ambitions of the 'Apiru Chief' Labaya of Shechem, who, however, was killed in a skirmish with loyalist forces.[2] He was succeeded by his sons, who proved no less fractious.[3] Towards the end of the reign unrest at Gezer imperilled the whole Egyptian position in Central Palestine, and it would seem that forces and supplies were being marshalled for a more serious campaign which may have been mounted early in the reign of Tutankhamun.[4] Whatever threat may have developed to the Egyptian position here, it had evidently been dispersed by the time Sethos I set out on his first foreign campaign, and there is no reason to doubt that under the successors of Akhenaten Palestine was as firmly held as it had ever been, despite the fissiparous nature of its politics, the constant jockeying for power by its princelings and the disorder caused by the operations of the Shasu and the Apiru.

Nubians and Kushites are represented on the monuments as equally prostrate beneath the feet of pharaoh as the Asiatics or the adoring *rekhyt* populace of Egypt, but during the greater part of the Eighteenth Dynasty the African dependencies were peaceful and well-ordered, being governed through an administration modelled on that of Egypt itself.[5] Punitive expeditions against nomad disturbers of the peace on the unsettled borders were undertaken by the Viceroys of Kush as part of their duties and were no more than police actions.[6] The processions of manacled prisoners in some of the representations of the time give a misleading picture of events in Africa, since these captives are often not prisoners of war, but the traditional 'black ivory' of the region, captured in slave-raids or trafficked together with the

---

[1] *C.A.H.* II^2, ch. xxi(*b*), 12; §iv, 4, 36.
[2] *C.A.H.* II^2, ch. xx, 20; §i, 5, 104, 110.
[3] *Ibid.* 103, 109; E.A. 289, 5; E.A. 287, 29–31.
[4] §vii, 8, 63–4.
[5] *C.A.H.* II^2, ch. ix, pt. 1, 38–40; §G, 12, 186 ff.
[6] *Ibid.* 162–7.

elephant tusks, ebony logs and gold dust as part of the native produce. The visit of Heknufer, the Prince of Miʿam (Aniba), and the Sudani princess with their retinues to the court of Tutankhamun, presumably at his accession, as represented in the tomb of the Viceroy Huy,[1] is a peaceful occasion and not a scene of conquest.[2] Similarly the victory over Kush depicted in the *speos* of Horemheb at Gebel es-Silsila is doubtless pure bombast, if it is not merely heraldic, showing the pharaoh as all-conquering in his southern domains as elsewhere.[3] If it has any basis in historical reality, it almost certainly refers to slave-raids or police action undertaken by the viceroys in his name.

The reliefs on the east wall of the court between the Ninth and Tenth Pylons at Karnak, showing delegates from Punt bringing gifts to Horemheb,[4] may, however, represent an historical event, since here the Puntites are hardly likely to represent the southern peoples in an equipoise of the foreign nations that owed allegiance to the pharaoh. This scene may therefore indicate that at the end of the Eighteenth Dynasty trading relations with the mysterious spice-lands of Punt had once more been re-established.

VIII. RELIGION, LITERATURE AND ART

A feature of religious thought during the Eighteenth Dynasty is a preponderance in the influence of the sun-cult, whose centre at Heliopolis, the Biblical On, was the chief seat of its theologians. These traditional 'wise men' of Egypt had radically overhauled their doctrines and re-interpreted old beliefs, perhaps as a result of seminal ideas from other sun-cults imported from Asia in Hyksos times.[5] The interpenetration of the new thought can be seen not only in the solarization of the old cults, which hastened to add the name of the supreme sun-god Re to the name of their local divinity, but also in the royal tombs at Thebes where the Pyramid Texts used in the Old and Middle Kingdoms were replaced by extracts from such sacred works as *The Book of What is in the Underworld*, *The Litany of the Sun* and *The Book of Gates*.[6] In these writings a new interest is revealed in a monotheistic syncretism of ancient beliefs. In them Re becomes the sole god who has made himself for eternity. He is invoked in *The Litany* under his 'seventy-five names which are his bodies, and these

---

[1] §IV, 9, pls. XXVII, XXVIII. [2] §VII, 3, 115.
[3] G, 11, V, 211(34)–(36); *cf.* G, 12, 107–8, 163 ff.
[4] G, 11, II, 61 (56). [5] §VIII, 8, 113–14.
[6] §VIII, 30, 121–2.

bodies are the other gods'.[1] He is hailed as 'the sole god who has made myriads from himself: all gods came into being from him'.[2] He is also invoked as 'he whose active forms are his eternal transformations when he assumes the aspect of his Great Disk'.[3] This disk, or *Aten*, which illumines the world of the dead as well as the living, and daily brings both to life from death or sleep,[4] is the constant element in these transformations, and the power immanent in it, Re, is the supreme god of whom the pharaoh is the offspring on earth.

The sun-worship of Akhenaten, which most modern observers have accepted as a new and revolutionary religion, differed from these re-edited doctrines of the Re-cult by a mere nuance, by placing a little more emphasis upon the Aten, or visible manifestation of godhead, than upon Re, the hidden power that motivated it.[5] It would seem that, as far as theological thought was concerned, there was little to choose between Atenism and the cults that it displaced. Amon-Re, the influential god of the dynasty, for instance, was also a 'hidden' force like Re, who might manifest himself in some tangible form, *e.g.* a ram (*cf.* the Mnevis bull of Re) rather than a remote and celestial body like the sun-disk. But his identification with Re weakened his ancient primal aspect of an ithyphallic god of storm, air and fertility, like his counterpart Min of the Eastern Desert, and he became purely the sun-god under the name of the god of Thebes, sailing over the waters above the earth in a divine bark, contending with the cloud-dragon Apophis and being worshipped as the creator and sustainer of all living things.[6] In Papyrus Bulaq 17, written about the time of Amenophis II,[7] all these aspects are praised in terms which differ little from similar phrases in the Great Hymn to the Aten, and it is doubtful whether a devotee of Amun of Thebes in the reign of Akhenaten would have found anything heretical in the doctrines being propounded by the new prophet at Akhetaten. In fact there is evidence that the personnel required for staffing the temples of the Aten at Karnak were drawn initially, at least, from the priesthood of Amun.[8]

Kings from the time of Ammenemes I had been spoken of as departing at death to the horizon and uniting with the Aten.[9] In

---

[1] §viii, 31, 207–8.   [2] *Ibid.* 208 n. 5.   [3] *Ibid.*
[4] §viii, 16, 21 ff.   [5] §viii, 31, 218; §iv, 26, 12–13.
[6] §viii, 18, 49 ff.; §viii, 29, 7–14; §viii, 41, 35; §ii, 12, 87.
[7] §viii, 34, 365–7.
[8] §viii, 25, 5, 6 n. 1; G, 13, 1935, l. 18; §vi, 5, 390–1.
[9] *Sinuhe*, R, 7; *cf.* G, 13, 54.

the reign of Amenophis II a symbol of the sun-disk had appeared with a pair of embracing arms,[1] and under Tuthmosis IV the Aten is mentioned on a scarab as a great universal god whose exalted position in the sky entitles it to rule over all that it shines upon.[2] In the reign of Amenophis III it became even more important, being attached to the name of the king's palace, his state-barge and one at least of his children, if not of himself.[3] Under Akhenaten, this deity became the supreme state-god, gradually achieving the position of a heavenly pharaoh who, like his earthly counterpart, had his names inscribed in two cartouches, assumed titles and epithets and celebrated jubilees. Where the Aten of Akhenaten differed from the Re of the new sacred books was that, instead of incorporating all the old deities in a comprehensive henotheism, it rigidly excluded them in an uncompromising monotheism.[4] This is seen as early as the Great Hymn to the Aten inscribed in the tomb of Ay before Year 9.[5] In this work, which has often been compared with Psalm 104, sentiments and phrases are included which can be found in earlier hymns to Amun and Osiris; where it differs from them is in ignoring completely the existence of other deities.

Later in the reign of Akhenaten this passive disregard of the other gods changed to an active antagonism which manifested itself in the excision of their names wherever they appeared, and the changing of the word for 'gods' to its singular form only. Just as remarkable, also, is the complete neglect of the old mortuary cults such as that of Osiris, with whom dead kings had become identified, and which had enjoyed an enormous expansion since the end of the Old Kingdom. The sun-god and his incarnation, the pharaoh, had taken over the care of the dead, and the new eschatology is seen in such features as changes in burial customs and funerary furnishings and the excision of the old *setem*-priest from the scenes of the last Osirian rites before entombment.[6] It is perhaps significant that special emphasis should have been placed upon the restoration of this scene in the wall-paintings in the tomb of Tutankhamun, where Ay officiates at the burial of his predecessor.[7]

---

[1] §VIII, 27, 53 ff.   [2] *C.A.H.* II², ch. IX, pt. 1, 33.
[3] §I, 10, 179; §III, 13, Pt. III, pl. XVIII; §III, 35, 33; §III, 19, 108; §VI, 2, pls. XXX–XXXI; §I, 18, 164, no. 13.
[4] G, 3, 63; G, 6, 227.
[5] §III, 13, Pt. VI, pl. XXVII; §VIII, 34, 369–71; G, 6, 225–7.
[6] §VIII, 16, 24–5; §VIII, 22, 21, 24, 58.
[7] See above, p. 23, n. 3.

Where Akhenaten's ideas of monotheism came from in a world which widely tolerated so many diverse forms of godhead is unknown, but the inference is that they were his own, the logical outcome of regarding the Aten as a heavenly king, whose son was the pharaoh. Like the latter, he could only be regarded as 'unique, without a peer'. It was, as has already been stated, the insistence by Akhenaten on a rigid monotheism in state affairs which proved disastrous for Egypt, since it destroyed the old system by which the lives of all the populace, from the lowest to the highest, had been regulated. In the world of the Late Bronze Age, religion and government were as inextricably mixed as they had ever been.

On the return to orthodoxy initiated by Akhenaten's successors, the old gods improved their position by the force of reaction, and that 'pagan' delight in the sunlit world of the living was in the ensuing dynasty to be excluded from the scenes painted on the walls of private tomb-chapels.[1] Nevertheless, it is probable that the faith of the mass of the Egyptian people was untouched by Akhenaten's religious reforms. They evidently continued to worship their old gods and godlings in the manner of their ancestors, for references to Bes, Toeris, Shed, Isis and even Amun were found in the workmen's village at El-Amarna.[2] The prayers and appeals of such humble folk, which show that a direct personal relationship was felt to exist between the petitioner and his god, are in marked contrast with the optimistic and complacent utterances of the official religion.[3] This spirit of self-abasement is more Hebraic than Egyptian in its concept of a merciful god who forgives the transgressor, and it may have owed something to the influence of the many Semites who had found an occupation in Egypt during the Eighteenth Dynasty. What has been called 'the religion of the poor' is better known from prayers written by the workmen at Thebes in Ramesside times,[4] but examples exist to show that such humble petitions were already being made as early as the reign of Amenophis III.[5]

Such minor compositions have often by their very unobtrusiveness survived unscathed the passage of time, but it is one of the ironies of chance that the Eighteenth Dynasty, which was one of the most prolific and imaginative periods of Egyptian art, has bequeathed us scarcely anything of its great literature. Hints exist in fragments of a story about the insatiable greed of the

---

[1] §I, 20, 226.
[2] §III, 32, 25, 60, 65–6, 95–8.
[3] *C.A.H.* II², ch. XXIII, 34.
[4] §VIII, 26, 87 ff.
[5] §VIII, 23, 188 ff.; *cf.* §IV, 18, 10–11.

sea,¹ a book on the pleasures of marsh sports and a poem on the joys of spring,² to suggest that the elegance, good proportions and high technical accomplishment of the plastic arts would have found their counterparts in contemporary writing; if so, it was a style of composition that made little appeal to the schoolboy copyists, or rather their teachers, whose scribbles have bequeathed us almost all that we now possess of earlier Egyptian literature.³ Nothing original exists, moreover, of the sapiential writings of Amenophis son of Hapu, whose wise sayings were treasured throughout the centuries, though a fragment of the *Instruction of Amonnakhte*⁴ shows that this class of wisdom literature was not neglected in the Dynasty.

That literary composition was moulded by the same influences that shaped the progress of the other arts is suggested by the utterances inscribed in the temple of Queen Hatshepsut at Deir el-Bahri accompanying reliefs inspired by Theban models of the early Middle Kingdom, and quoting from the classical *Story of Sinuhe*.⁵ As the dynasty wears on and art becomes freer, its lines more flowing and its compositions more adventurous, particularly in such a non-royal genre as the paintings in the private tomb-chapels at Thebes, the language also changes to express a more flexible and vernacular manner of speech. New grammatical tendencies and idioms, foreign words and a different orthography characteristic of Late Egyptian began to replace classical Middle Egyptian about the reign of Tuthmosis III for less formal writings, but at El-Amarna they had already entered the monumental texts.⁶

It is from its official inscriptions, in fact, that any appreciation of the literary achievement of the Eighteenth Dynasty has to be gleaned. The Annals of Tuthmosis III, inscribed on walls adjacent to the innermost shrine of the temple of Amun at Karnak, are remarkable for their terse, methodical record of events, with so little of the bombast that passes for the writing of history in ancient Egypt that they can be accepted with some confidence.⁷ The stelae which describe the Homeric prowess of the pharaohs as sportsmen also, in their vivid hyperbole and the elegance of their diction, are surely indicative of a not unhappy striving on the part of their authors for a literary excellence which

---

¹ §VIII, 24, 74 ff.; §VIII, 32, 461 ff.
² §VIII, 9, 1–21; §VIII, 17, 252–3; §VIII, 12, pl. LXX.
³ *Ibid.* 185 ff.   ⁴ §VIII, 33, 61 ff.
⁵ §VIII, 17, 14 n. 4.   ⁶ *E.g.* §II, 13, 220–1.
⁷ G, 13, 645–756; G, 1, vol. II, §§407–540.

RELIGION, LITERATURE AND ART

would match the marvellous feats of the royal paragons.[1] By the end of the dynasty literary artifice had almost triumphed over clarity of expression, as in the Coronation Inscription of Horemheb, where the historical facts of his accession have been obscured by elaborate flowers of speech.[2] This may, however, be a deliberate glossing over of the means by which the king attained a throne to which he had no strong claim.

Such records are the prose of the period. The poetry has to be sought in the hymns written to Amun of Thebes and the Aten of Akhetaten. The great triumphal hymn celebrating the victorious might of Tuthmosis III, inscribed on a magnificent stela of polished black granite from Karnak,[3] contains an apostrophe by Amun which is clearly cast in a poetical form, the balanced strophes being emphasized by the disposition of the hieroglyphs:

I have come
    that I may cause thee to trample upon the great ones of Phoenicia; that I may strew them under thy feet throughout their lands; that I may cause them to see thy Majesty as the Lord of Radiance,
        when thou shinest in their sight like my image.

I have come
    that I may cause thee to trample upon them that are in Asia; that thou mayest strike the heads of the Asiatics of Syria; that I may cause them to see thy Majesty equipped with thy panoply
        when thou seizest the weapons in thy chariot. . .

This composition was evidently considered a masterpiece, for phrases from it inspired similar triumphal hymns written for later kings.[4] Thus Amenophis III set up a great black granite stela at Medînet Habu which recounted his achievements based upon a phrase taken from the earlier inscription:

I turn my face towards the south,
    that I may perform a wonder for thee;
causing the great ones of Kush to
    hasten to thee bearing all their gifts upon their shoulders.

I turn my face towards the north,
    that I may perform a wonder for thee;
causing the nations to come from the ends of Asia,
bearing their gifts upon their shoulders and giving
themselves to thee, together with their children,
that thou mayest grant them in return the breath of life.[5]

---

[1] §VIII, 34, 243–5; *C.A.H.* II², ch. IX, pt. I, p. 23.
[2] §V, 10, 21.
[3] G, 9, no. 34010; G, 13, 610–19; §VIII, 34, 373–5.
[4] *Ibid.* 373.   [5] G, 9, no. 34025; §VIII, 34, 375–6.

The hymn to Amun written on Papyrus Bulaq 17 has already been mentioned as a forerunner of the Great Hymn to the Aten. In it Amun is hailed as a pharaoh and in phrases that recall those of the later hymn is referred to as 'the Solitary One with many hands, the Sole One who made all that exists' and is identified with the Creator 'who made mankind, distinguished their nature and made their life...Who made that on which the fish in the river may live and the birds soaring in the sky...Who gives breath to that which is in the egg and gives life to the offspring of the worm.'[1] The Great Hymn to the Aten, however, is justly praised as the masterpiece of psalmodic writing in the Eighteenth Dynasty, and its unknown author is often identified as Akhenaten himself, though it should be noted that the only known full-length copy appears in the Amarna tomb of Ay.[2] Many of its sentiments can be paralleled in other hymns, as has been mentioned, but the organic succession of its thought and expression demonstrates the difference between the mechanical stringing together of resounding phrases, culled from a corpus of such passages, and the inspired work of a true poet:[3]

Thou it is who causeth women to conceive and maketh seed into man; who giveth life to the child in the womb of its mother; who comforteth him so that he cries not therein, nurse that thou art, even in the womb! Who giveth breath to quicken all that he hath made.

When the child cometh forth from the womb on the day of his birth, then thou openest his mouth completely and thou furnishest his sustenance.

When the chicken in the egg chirps within the shell, thou givest him the breath within it to sustain him. Thou createst for him his proper term within the egg...

How manifold are thy works! They are hidden from the sight of men, O Sole God, like unto whom there is no other!

We shall have occasion to observe the same sensibility at work in the creation of Amarna pictorial art, where a unified composition replaces the old assemblage of diverse parts. Some of the shorter hymns at Amarna also contain passages of poetic beauty, particularly in their loyal praise of Akhenaten and his queen,[4] and the same original phraseology is found in the substitutes for the old Osirian funeral formulae. A notable example of this is the prayer on the foot-board of the coffin in which Smenkhkare was buried, but which originally was made for a daughter of Akhenaten,[5] who addresses him thus:

[1] *Ibid.* 365–7; §viii, 17, 282–8. [2] See above, p. 45, n. 5. [3] §ii, 12, 90.
[4] §iii, 13, Pt. i, pl. xxxvi; Pt. ii, pl. xxxvi; Pt. iii, pl. xxix; Pt. vi, pl. xxv.
[5] §iv, 17, 35–6.

I shall breathe the sweet air that issues from thy mouth. My prayer is that I may behold thy beauty daily; that I may hear thy sweet voice belonging to the North Wind; that my body may grow young with life through thy love; that thou mayest give me thy hands bearing thy sustenance and I receive it and live by it; and that thou mayest call upon my name for ever and it shall not fail in thy mouth.

The modernization of Amarna hymnody is here complete. Instead of the conjuration of the god by his suppliant with propitiatory praises that had varied little since archaic times, the relationship of worshipper to deity is one of mutual affection. It is perhaps significant that this prayer of a faith that spoke much of love[1] should contain sentiments which find their echo in the secular love poetry of the following dynasty, though the fragment from the tomb of Nebamun in the British Museum[2] shows that some of it could have been composed in the Eighteenth Dynasty.

The same vulgarization is seen in the plastic arts which, during the reign of Amenophis III, were characterized by the weakening of the idealism of the official style in favour of a more sensuous naturalism. The rather prim and precise drawing of the reigns of Tuthmosis III and Amenophis II is replaced by a more dashing line and adventurous use of colour, though the craftsmanship is still meticulous.[3] The change is most marked in the last decade of the reign, by which time a new generation of artists must have succeeded their fathers.[4] The sculpture of this period is much more realistic. The torsos of the king found at Medīnet Habu and the statuette in New York[5] show him in all the obesity of his later years, while the little head of Tiy from Sinai is no less frank in revealing her features as sharp and lined.[6] At the same time iconography is brought up to date to reveal fashions of dress that had replaced the traditional garments of both kings and commoners. This tendency towards 'modernism' continues unabated in the reign of Akhenaten and is found in such stylistic details as a more natural setting of the eye within its socket, the delineation of the lines that run from the corners of the eyes and nose, the folds in the neck, the large perforations in the ear-lobes and the contemporary modes of dressing the hair.[7] The inno-

---

[1] §III, 13, Pt. I, 45; §V, 5, 8.
[2] §VIII, 12, pl. LXX; §VIII, 17, 252–3.
[3] Cf. §VIII, 12, pls. XVII, XXXV, XXXVI, LII, LXI, LXX.
[4] §VIII, 3, 78.   [5] See above, p. 5, n. 2.
[6] §VIII, 2, nos. 83, 84; §II, 2, pls. 21, 22.
[7] §VIII, 1, 141 ff.; cf. §VIII, 21, 29 n. 3. This stela (G, 9, no. 34023), however, is a posthumous representation of Tuthmosis IV belonging to a later period in the dynasty.

vations, however, were not accepted wholesale, and the finished reliefs in the tomb of the vizier Ramose at Thebes and one or two statues of private persons are completely in the style of the preceding reign.[1]

The great departure of Akhenaten's reign, however, and the one that has been responsible for accrediting him with a new 'realism' in Egyptian art, is his choosing to have his family and himself represented as though they suffered from some physical abnormality. Akhenaten's faithful courtiers followed his example in claiming similar diseased physiques, though the common folk were spared such marks of the elect. The distortion that Egyptian drawing now underwent is so gross as to verge on crude caricature in its more extreme and less accomplished examples,[2] but it cannot be denied that the colossal statues from Karnak, presumably the work of his master-sculptor Bak, still have a power to move the spectator by their inner spiritual malaise.[3] This revolutionary style erupts early in his reign, perhaps in his second regnal year, but it becomes more refined with the passage of time, presumably as his artists became more experienced and the less expert among them were replaced.

Apart from this new mannerism, Akhenaten inspired no fundamental change in age-old Egyptian conventions of drawing the human figure, but his artists did introduce a new space-concept in which to represent the new subjects for illustration which he must have specified. We have already remarked that in the Amarna tombs traditional themes for decoration are banished in favour of representations of events in the life of the royal family. During the dynasty there had been a steady growth in the popularity of a trinity consisting of a pair of deities and their male offspring, an idea that appealed particularly to the Egyptian with his strong love of family. This tendency received a considerable stimulus when the new sun-god could no longer be exhibited in iconic form, and scenes of religious import were replaced by compositions in which his incarnation in the person of the pharaoh with his wife and daughters enacted incidents from their lives—the worship of the Aten,[4] the investiture before the palace balcony,[5] the visit to the temple[6] and so forth.[7] Stelae used like triptychs in

[1] §III, 15, pls. XLVI–XLVIII; §VIII, 6, 79ff.; §VIII, 7, 167 (reg. no 69·45).
[2] §VIII, 13, 10; §IV, 14, 105.
[3] §II, 2, pls. 2–4; §VIII, 2, nos. 107–9; §IV, 14, pl. 95; §VIII, 28, pls. 176, 177.
[4] §III, 13, Pt. II, pls. V, VII, VIII; Pt. IV, pl. XXXI. See Plate Vol.
[5] *Ibid.* Pt. VI, pls. XXIX, XLII.   [6] *Ibid.* Pt. I, pl. XXV; Pt. III, pl. VIII.
[7] *E.g. ibid.* Pt. I, pl. X; Pt. II, pls. XVIII, XXXVII; Pt. III, pl. XXXIIA; Pt. IV, pl. VI; Pt. VI, pl. VI.

RELIGION, LITERATURE AND ART

the chapels connected with private houses show the royal family in even more intimate scenes with the queen seated in the king's lap, or playing with their children.[1]

There were no precedents in Egyptian religious art for such subjects, and the artists therefore took their inspiration from the vernacular art that had already appeared in the scenes of everyday life in the Theban tomb-paintings. The royal family and the courtiers are now grouped in the same poses that had hitherto been reserved for the lowly and the vulgar.[2] They express emotions of unction, joy, pride and sorrow not by a symbolic gesture, but by pose and facial expression, like the mourners before the tomb-door or the dancers at the feast.[3]

These new subjects are depicted in a novel manner in the Amarna tomb-reliefs. Instead of a selection of standard scenes taken from pattern-books and assembled haphazardly according to the taste of the patron, each wall of the chamber is considered a complete entity and decorated with a single composition. Indeed, in a chamber in the royal tomb, one scene is spread over two adjacent walls.[4] A room in the Northern Palace was decorated apparently with one continuous scene of bird-life among the papyrus thickets.[5] The same readiness to regard space as a totality is revealed in the sarcophagus of Tutankhamun, where the goddesses stand at the corners, each with her spine in alignment with the edge where two adjacent sides meet.[6] The disposition of Nefertiti on a fragment of a corner of a sarcophagus from the royal tomb shows that this pose was an innovation of the preceding reign.[7] That it was felt to be outside the natural instincts of the Egyptian artist is seen in the similar sarcophagus of Horemheb, where the four goddesses have been so placed that two are fully revealed on each long side, one only of their winged arms being on each short end.[8] Nevertheless, many of the Amarna novelties remained in the repertoire of Egyptian art-forms, such as the 'caryatid' figures of the pharaoh standing against a pillar in the costume of the living[9] and the decoration of Ramesside walls and pylons.[10] In the unified compositions of Amarna art we can see at work the same influences that are

---

[1] §III, 35, pl. I, 16; §VIII, 13, pls. 8, 9, 11; §VIII, 40, pl. 22; §VIII, 35, pl. 51.
[2] *Cf.* §VIII, 11, 29; §VIII, 28, 147.
[3] §VIII, 21, 8, 9; §VIII, 10, 11–12. [4] §III, 9, pl. I.
[5] §VIII, 21, 58–9. [6] §VIII, 2, no. 161.
[7] §III, 38, 5; §VIII, 40, pl. 56.
[8] §II, 2, pl. III; §V, 6, pls. LXV, LXVIII, LXXIII.
[9] As, for instance, in the first courts of the great temples at Abu Simbel and Medīnet Habu (Ramesses III). [10] §I, 20, 209, 222–4.

manifest in a monotheistic conception of godhead and in the progression of thought in the Great Hymn to the Aten, although such tendencies are already present in the reign of Amenophis III.[1]

The excesses of the earlier Karnak style, still evident in the Boundary Stelae and other reliefs from Amarna, had been modified by the later years of Akhenaten, though the casts found in the sculptors' studios at El-Amarna tend to give an unbalanced view of the 'naturalism' of the period, since for the most part they appear to be portrait studies modelled from the life in wax or clay to catch a likeness and be cast in plaster for working over to an accepted standard.[2] To this period belongs the famous painted bust of Nefertiti modelled in plaster over a limestone core.[3]

This restrained style was more sympathetic to the temper of the post-Amarna age when a return was made to the traditions of Amenophis III, though the artists did not discard all they had been allowed to express under Akhenaten. The statuary of the end of the dynasty is among the finest produced in its noble proportions, high technical excellence and the individualism of its portraiture.[4] A group of sculptors working at Memphis produced reliefs for the private tombs, notably that of Horemheb, which show the same qualities in their lively scenes, splendidly conceived and executed.[5] These are among the last expressions of that delight in the world of the living and pride in worldly success which is the special contribution of the Eighteenth Dynasty to Egyptian art.

The decoration of tomb walls at El-Amarna and Memphis with carved reliefs broke the traditions of the Theban tomb-painters and they never recovered the assurance and mastery that they had demonstrated under Amenophis III. The painting in the tomb of Huy and others is often poor in its drawing and proportions and crude in its colouring, and many of the mannerisms of the Ramesside style are already anticipated.[6] The same loss of confidence is seen in the wall-paintings in the tombs of Tutankhamun and Ay.[7]

The Amarna age showed no falling-off in its appetite for exotic objects of great luxury, particularly in gold, glass and polychrome

---

[1] Cf. scenes of the owner before his king in Theban tombs nos. 48 and 57, G, 11, 1², Pt. II, p. 88 (4), 89 (7); p. 115 (11), 116 (15).   [2] §VIII, 36, 145 ff.
[3] §VIII, 5; §VIII, 4; §VIII, 13, pls. 13, 14; §II, 2, pls. VIII, 7.
[4] E.g. §II, 2, pls. 56, 63–6; §VIII, 13, pls. 7, 24; §VIII, 28, pls. 196–9; §VIII, 2, no. 175.
[5] §VIII, 2, nos. 144–8; §V, 3, pls. V–VII; §VIII, 13, pls. 4, 5, 22, 23, 27–31.
[6] §IV, 9, 3; §I, 20, 210.   [7] §IV, 25; §IV, 29.

faïence, that had characterized the reign of Amenophis III. The specimens found in the tomb of Tutankhamun give an unparalleled conspectus of the applied arts of the period, and while some of them seem hasty in execution and over-exuberant in taste, certain items may be singled out for their high technical excellence, such as some of the wooden furniture, an ivory bracelet exquisitely carved in coin-like relief with a frieze of horses, and the great head-rest of rich blue glass.[1] A novelty of the age is the gold tinted in tones from pink to purple by a metallurgical process,[2] but as Tushratta of the Mitanni speaks of sending the pharaoh gold ornaments 'through which blood shines',[3] we may presume this to have been an Asiatic invention, like his iron dagger-blade.[4]

[1] §IV, 5, vol. I, pl. XLIX; §VIII, 14, pls. XII, XLIA, L.
[2] *Ibid.* pl. XXIIA.
[3] E.A. 22, I, ll. 20, 25; II, ll. 8, 15.
[4] E.A. 22, I, l. 32; II, l. 16; III, l. 7; §VIII, 14, pl. XXIB; §IV, 5, vol. II, 135-6.

BIBLIOGRAPHY

G. GENERAL

1. Breasted, J. H. *Ancient Records of Egypt: Historical Documents* (*Ancient Records*, 2nd Series), 2: *The Eighteenth Dynasty.* 3: *The Nineteenth Dynasty.* Chicago, 1906.
2. Breasted, J. H. *A History of Egypt from the Earliest Times to the Persian Conquest.* Ed. 2. London, 1948.
3. Černý, J. *Ancient Egyptian Religion.* London, 1952.
4. Drioton, É. and Vandier, J. *L'Égypte* (Clio: *Les peuples de l'Orient méditerranéen*, 2). Ed. 4. Paris, 1962, pp. 343-55, 367-9, 373-5, 384-6, 414-18, 446-7.
5. Gardiner, A. H. *Ancient Egyptian Onomastica.* 3 vols. Oxford, 1947.
6. Gardiner, A. H. *Egypt of the Pharaohs.* Oxford, 1961.
7. Hayes, W. C. *The Scepter of Egypt.* Part 2. New York, 1959.
8. Kees, H. *Ancient Egypt, A Cultural Topography.* Ed. T. G. H. James. London, 1961.
9. Lacau, P. *Stèles du Nouvel Empire* (C.C.G. nos. 34001-189). Cairo, 1909-57.
10. Petrie, W. M. F. *A History of Egypt*, II. *The XVIIth and XVIIIth Dynasties.* Ed. 7. London, 1924.
11. Porter, B. and Moss, R. L. B. *Topographical Bibliography of Ancient Egyptian Hieroglyphic Texts, Reliefs and Paintings.* 7 vols. Oxford, 1927-64.
12. Säve-Söderbergh, T. *Ägypten und Nubien. Ein Beitrag zur Geschichte altägyptischer Aussenpolitik.* Lund, 1941.
13. Sethe, K. and Helck, H.-W. *Urkunden der 18 Dynastie* (*Urk. IV*). Hefte 1-22. Leipzig and Berlin, 1906-58.
14. Smith, G. E. *The Royal Mummies* (C.C.G. nos. 61051-100). Cairo, 1912.
15. Thomas, E. *The Royal Necropoleis of Thebes.* Princeton, 1966.
16. Waddell, W. G. *Manetho, with an English Translation* (The Loeb Classical Library). London and Cambridge (Mass.), 1940.

52 THE END OF THE EIGHTEENTH DYNASTY

I. THE PROBLEM OF A CO-REGENCY BETWEEN AMENOPHIS III AND AKHENATEN

1. Aldred, C. 'Year Twelve at El-'Amārna.' In *J.E.A.* 43 (1957), 30 ff.
2. Aldred, C. 'Two Theban Notables during the Later Reign of Amenophis III.' In *J.N.E.S.* 18 (1959), 113 ff.
3. Aldred, C. 'The Beginning of the El-Amārna Period.' In *J.E.A.* 45 (1959), 19 ff.
4. Aldred, C. *Akhenaten, Pharaoh of Egypt: A New Study*, Chapters VI, VII and XI. London, 1968.
5. Campbell, E. F. *The Chronology of the Amarna Letters*, Chapter II. Baltimore, 1964.
6. Drioton, É. and Vandier, J. *L'Égypte* (Clio: *Les peuples de l'Orient méditerranéen*, 2). Ed. 4. Paris, 1962. Pp. 384–6, 631, 658–61.
7. Engelbach, R. 'Material for a Revision of the History of the Heresy Period of the XVIIIth Dynasty.' In *Ann. Serv.* 40 (1940), 134 ff.
8. Fairman, H. W. 'A Block of Amenophis IV from Athribis.' In *J.E.A.* 46 (1960), 80 ff.
9. Gardiner, A. H. 'The So-called Tomb of Queen Tiye.' In *J.E.A.* 43 (1957), 10 ff.
10. Hayes, W. C. 'Inscriptions from the Palace of Amenophis III.' In *J.N.E.S.* 10 (1951).
11. Helck, H.-W. 'Die Sinai-Inschrift des Amenmose.' In *Mitt. Inst. Or.* 2 (1954), 189 ff.
12. Hornung, E. *Untersuchungen zur Chronologie und Geschichte des Neuen Reiches*, Chapter X. Wiesbaden, 1964.
13. Kitchen, K. A. 'On the Chronology and History of the New Kingdom.' In *Chron. d'Ég.* 40 (1965), 310 ff.
14. Kitchen, K. A. Review of E. F. Campbell, *The Chronology of the Amarna Letters.* In *J.E.A.* 53 (1967), 178 ff.
15. Kitchen, K. A. 'Further Notes on New Kingdom Chronology and History. In *Chron. d'Ég.* 43 (1968), 313 ff.
16. Pendlebury. J. D. S. *Tell el-Amarna.* London, 1935.
17. Pendlebury, J. D. S. 'Summary Report on Excavations at Tell el-'Amārnah, 1935–6.' In *J.E.A.* 22 (1936), 197–8.
18. Pendlebury, J. D. S. *et al. The City of Akhenaten*, Part III (E.E.S. 44th Memoir). 2 vols. London, 1951.
19. Redford, D. B. *History and Chronology of the Eighteenth Dynasty of Egypt: Seven Studies*, Chapter 5. Toronto, 1967.
20. Smith, W. S. *The Art and Architecture of Ancient Egypt.* Harmondsworth, 1958.
21. Wente, E. F. Review of D. B. Redford, *History and Chronology of the Eighteenth Dynasty.* In *J.N.E.S.* 28 (1969), 273 ff.

II. THE CHARACTER OF THE AMARNA 'REVOLUTION'

1. Aldred, C. 'The Beginning of the El-Amārna Period.' In *J.E.A.* 45 (1959), 19 ff.
2. Aldred, C. *Akhenaten, Pharaoh of Egypt: A New Study.* London, 1968.
3. Bothmer, B. V. 'A New Fragment of an Old Palette.' In *J.A.R.C.E.* 8 (1969), 1–4.

4. Breasted, J. H. *A History of Egypt from the Earliest Times to the Persian Conquest*. Ed. 2. London, 1948.
5. Cottevieille-Giraudet, R. *Rapport sur les fouilles de Médamoud, 1932. Les reliefs d'Amenophis IV Akhenaten* (*Flles. Inst. fr. Caire*, 13). Cairo, 1936.
6. Davis, T. M., Maspero, G. *et al. Tomb of Iouiya and Touiyou*. London, 1907.
7. Edgerton, W. F. 'The Government and the Governed in the Egyptian Empire.' In *J.N.E.S.* 6 (1947), 152 ff.
8. Fakhry, A. 'A Note on the Tomb of Kheruef at Thebes.' In *Ann. Serv.* 42 (1943), 447 ff.
9. Gardiner, A. H. *The Wilbour Papyrus*. 3 vols. Oxford, 1941–8. Vol. IV, Indices, by R. O. Faulkner. Oxford, 1952.
10. Gardiner, A. H. 'Ramesside Texts Relating to the Transport and Taxation of Corn.' In *J.E.A.* 27 (1941), 19 ff.
11. Petrie, W. M. F. *Royal Tombs of the Earliest Dynasties*. Part II (E.E.S. 21st Memoir). London, 1901.
12. Stewart, H. M. 'Some Pre-'Amārneh Sun-Hymns.' In *J.E.A.* 46 (1960), 83 ff.
13. Wilson, J. A. *The Burden of Egypt: An Interpretation of Ancient Egyptian Culture*. Chicago, 1951.

III. THE REIGN OF AKHENATEN

1. Aldred, C. 'The Gayer Anderson Jubilee Relief of Amenophis IV.' In *J.E.A.* 45 (1959), 104.
2. Aldred, C. and Sandison, A. T. 'The Tomb of Akhenaten at Thebes.' In *J.E.A.* 47 (1961), 41 ff.
3. Aldred, C. and Sandison, A. T. 'The Pharaoh Akhenaten: A Problem in Egyptology and Pathology.' In *Bull. Hist. Med.* 36 (1962), 293 ff.
4. Anthes, R. 'Die Maat des Echnaton von Amarna.' In *J.A.O.S.* 14 (Supplement) 1952, 1–36.
5. Badawy, A. 'Maru-Aten: Pleasure Resort or Temple.' In *J.E.A.* 42 (1956), 58 ff.
6. Bennett, J. 'Notes on the "aten".' In *J.E.A.* 51 (1965), 207 ff.
7. Bissing, F. W. von, *et al. Das Re-Heiligtum des Königs Ne-Woser-Re* (*Rathures*). 3 vols. Berlin and Leipzig, 1905–28.
8. Borchardt, L. 'Ausgrabungen in Tell el-Amarna.' In *M.D.O.G.* nos. 34, 46, 50, 52, 55 (1907–14).
9. Bouriant, U. *et al. Monuments pour servir à l'étude du culte d'Atonou en Égypte.* I. *Les tombes de Khouitatonou* (*Mém. Inst. fr.* Caire, 8). Cairo, 1903.
10. Bouriant, U. *Deux jours de fouilles à Tell el-Amarna* (*Mém. Miss. Arch. Fr.* I, I). Paris, 1884.
11. Brunner, H. 'Eine Neue Amarna-Prinzessin.' In *Z.Ä.S.* 74 (1938), 104 ff.
12. Chevrier, H. 'Rapport(s) sur les travaux de Karnak.' In *Ann. Serv.* 26–39 (1926–9) and 46–53 (1947–55) *passim*.
13. Davies, Norman de G. *The Rock Tombs of El Amarna*. 6 vols. London, 1903–8.
14. Davies, Norman de G. 'Akhenaten at Thebes.' In *J.E.A.* 9 (1923), 132 ff.
15. Davies, Norman de G. *The Tomb of the Vizier Ramose* (Mond Excavations at Thebes I). London, 1941.
16. Doresse, M. 'Les Temples Atoniens de la région thébaine.' In *Orientalia*, 24 (1955), 113 ff.

17. Fairman, H. W. 'Town Planning in Pharaonic Egypt.' In *Town Planning Review*, 20 (1949), 32 ff.
18. Fairman, H. W. 'The supposed Year 21 of Akhenaten.' In *J.E.A.* 46 (1960), 108 ff.
19. Frankfort, H., Pendlebury, J. D. S., et al. *The City of Akhenaten*, Part II (E.E.S. 40th Memoir). London, 1933.
20. Gardiner, A. H. 'Four Papyri of the 18th Dynasty from Kahun.' In *Z.Ä.S.* 43 (1906), 27 ff.
21. Gauthier, H. *Le Livre des rois d'Égypte*, II (*Mém. Inst. fr.* Caire, 18). Cairo, 1912.
22. Ghalioungui, P. 'A Medical Study of Akhenaten.' In *Ann. Serv.* 47 (1947), 29 ff.
23. Griffith, F. Ll. 'The Jubilee of the Aten.' In *J.E.A.* 5 (1918), 61 ff. Also *ibid.* 8 (1922), 199 ff.
24. Gunn, B. 'Notes on the Aten and his Names.' In *J.E.A.* 9 (1923), 168 ff.
25. Habachi, L. 'Varia from the Reign of King Akhenaten.' In *Mitt. deutsch. Inst. Kairo*, 20 (1965), 70 ff.
26. Hamza, M. 'The Alabaster Canopic Box of Akhenaten, and the Royal Alabaster Canopic Boxes of the XVIIIth Dynasty.' In *Ann. Serv.* 40 (1941), 537 ff.
27. Harrison, R. G. 'An Anatomical Examination of the Pharaonic Remains Purported to be Akhenaten.' In *J.E.A.* 52 (1966), 95 ff.
28. Kamal, M. 'Fouilles du Service des Antiquités à Tell el-Amarna.' In *Ann. Serv.* 35 (1935), 193 ff., and *ibid.* 39 (1939), 381 ff.
29. Lange, K. *König Echnaton und die Amarna-Zeit*. Munich, 1951.
30. Legrain, G. 'Notes d'Inspection: I. Les stèles d'Aménôthès IV à Zernik et à Gebel Silsileh.' In *Ann. Serv.* 3 (1902), 259 ff.
31. Monnet, J. 'Remarques sur la famille et les successeurs de Ramsès III.' In *Bull. Inst. fr. Caire*, 63 (1965), 209 ff.
32. Peet, T. E., Woolley, C. L., et al. *The City of Akhenaten*. Part I (E.E.S. 38th Memoir). London, 1923.
33. Pendlebury, J. D. S. 'Report on the clearance of the Royal Tomb at El-'Amârna.' In *Ann. Serv.* 21 (1931), 123–5.
34. Pendlebury, J. D. S. 'Preliminary Report[s] of Excavations at Tell el-'Amarnah 1930–33.' In *J.E.A.* 17 (1931), 233 ff.; 18 (1932), 143 ff.; 19 (1933), 113 ff.
35. Petrie, W. M. F. *Tell el-Amarna*. London, 1894.
36. Reymond, E. A. E. *The Mythical Origin of the Egyptian Temple*. Manchester, 1969.
37. Roeder, G. *Ein Jahrzehnt deutscher Ausgrabungen in einer ägyptischen Stadtruine*. Hildesheim, 1951.
38. Schäfer, H. 'Altes und Neues zur Kunst und Religion von Tell el-Amarna.' In *Z.Ä.S.* 55 (1918), 1 ff.
39. Schäfer, H. 'Das Wesen der "Amarnakunst".' In *Mitt. deutsch. Orient. Gesellft.* 64 (1926), 54–61.
40. Sethe, K. *Beiträge zur Geschichte Amenophis IV.* (Nachrichten der königliche Gesellschaft der Wissenschaften zu Göttingen, Phil.-hist. Klasse, 1921). Berlin, 1921.
41. Smith, R. W. 'The Akhenaten Temple Project.' In *Expedition* (*Bull. Univ. Mus. Penna.*), 10, No. 1 (1967), 24–32.
42. Uphill, E. 'The Sed-Festivals of Akhenaten.' In *J.N.E.S.* 22 (1963), 123 ff.

IV. THE IMMEDIATE SUCCESSORS OF AKHENATEN

1. Aldred, C. 'The Harold Jones Collection.' In *J.E.A.* 48 (1962), 160–2.
2. Bennett, J. 'The Restoration Inscription of Tut'ankhamūn.' In *J.E.A.* 25 (1939), 8 ff.
3. Blackman, A. M. 'The Haggard Collection.' In *J.E.A.* 4 (1917), 43 ff.
4. Bosse-Griffiths, K. 'Finds from "the Tomb of Queen Tiye" in the Swansea Museum.' In *J.E.A.* 47 (1961), 66 ff.
5. Carter, H., et al. *The Tomb of Tut.Ankh.Amen.* 3 vols. London, 1923–33.
6. Černý, J. *Hieratic Inscriptions from the Tomb of Tut'ankhamūn.* Oxford, 1965.
7. Černý, J. 'Three Regnal Dates of the Eighteenth Dynasty.' In *J.E.A.* 50 (1964), 37 ff.
8. Daressy, G. 'Le Cercueil de Khu-n-Aten.' In *Bull. Inst. fr. Caire*, 12 (1916), 145 ff.
9. Davies, Nina de G. and Gardiner, A. H. *The Tomb of Huy, Viceroy of Nubia in the Reign of Tut'ankhamun.* London, 1926.
10. Davies, Norman de G. *The Tomb of Nefer-Ḥotep at Thebes.* 2 vols. New York, 1933.
11. Davis, T. M., Maspero, G., et al. *The Tomb of Queen Tîyi.* London, 1910.
12. Derry, D. 'Note on the Skeleton hitherto believed to be that of King Akhenaten.' In *Ann. Serv.* 31 (1931), 115 ff.
13. Desroches-Noblecourt, C. 'La Cueillette du Raisin à la Fin de l'Époque amarnienne.' In *J.E.A.* 54 (1968), 82 ff.
14. Drioton, É., and Vigneau, A. *Encyclopédie Photographique de l'Art: Le Musée du Caire.* Editions 'Tel'. Paris, 1949.
15. Edwards, I. E. S. 'The Prudhoe Lions.' In *Ann. Arch. Anthr.* 26 (1939), 3 ff.
16. Engelbach, R. 'The So-called Coffin of Akhenaten.' In *Ann. Serv.* 31 (1931), 98 ff.
17. Fairman, H. W. 'Once again the So-called Coffin of Akhenaten.' In *J.E.A.* 47 (1961), 25 ff.
18. Gardiner, A. H. 'The Graffito in the Tomb of Pere.' In *J.E.A.* 14 (1928), 10–11.
19. Gardiner, A. H. 'Regnal Years and the Civil Calendar in Pharaonic Egypt.' In *J.E.A.* 31 (1945), 11 ff.
20. Gardiner, A. H. 'The So-called Tomb of Queen Tiye.' In *J.E.A.* 43 (1957), 10 ff.
21. Hall, H. R. 'Objects of Tut'ankhamūn in the British Museum.' In *J.E.A.* 14 (1928), 74 ff.
22. Lucas, A. 'The Canopic Vases from the "Tomb of Queen Tîyi".' In *Ann. Serv.* 31 (1931), 120 ff.
23. Newberry, P. E. 'Akhenaten's Eldest Son-in-Law.' In *J.E.A.* 14 (1928), 3 ff.
24. Newberry, P. E. 'King Ay, the Successor of Tut'ankhamūn.' In *J.E.A.* 18 (1932), 50 ff.
25. Piankoff, A. 'Les Peintures dans la Tombe du roi Ai.' In *Mitt. deutsch. Inst. Kairo*, 16 (1958), 247 ff.
26. Piankoff, A. *The Shrines of Tut-Ankh-Amon.* New York, 1962.
27. Roeder, G. 'Thronfolger und König Smench-ka-Rê.' In *Z.Ä.S.* 83 (1958), 43 ff.

28. Seele, K. C. 'King Ay and the Close of the Amarna Age.' In *J.N.E.S.* 14 (1955), 168 ff.
29. Steindorff, G. 'Die Grabkammer des Tutanchamun.' In *Ann. Serv.* 38 (1938), 641 ff.
30. Vilimkova, M. and Abdu-Rahman, M. H. *Egyptian Jewellery*. London, 1969. Pls. 32–67.
31. Weigall, A. 'The Mummy of Akhenaten.' In *J.E.A.* 8 (1922), 193 ff.

V. THE REIGN OF HOREMHEB

1. Aldred, C. 'Two Monuments of the Reign of Ḥaremḥab.' In *J.E.A.* 54 (1968), 100 ff.
2. Breasted, J. H. 'King Harmhab and his Sakkara Tomb.' In *Z.Ä.S.* 38 (1900), 47 ff.
3. Capart, J. 'The Memphite Tomb of King Ḥaremḥab.' In *J.E.A.* 7 (1921), 31 ff.
4. Carter, H. and Newberry, P. E. *The Tomb of Thoutmôsis IV* (*C.C.G.* nos. 46001–529). London, 1904.
5. Cooney, J. D. 'A Relief from the Tomb of Ḥaremḥab.' In *J.E.A.* 30 (1944), 2–4.
6. Davis, T. M., Maspero, G. *et al. The Tombs of Harmhabi and Touatânkhamanou*. London, 1912.
7. Erman, A. 'Aus dem Grabe eines Hohenpriesters von Memphis.' In *Z.Ä.S.* 33 (1895), 18 ff.
8. Gardiner, A. H. *The Inscription of Mes. A Contribution to the Study of Egyptian Judicial Procedure.* (*Unters., IV, 3.*) Leipzig, 1905.
9. Gardiner, A. H. 'The Memphite Tomb of the General Ḥaremḥab.' In *J.E.A.* 39 (1953), 3 ff.
10. Gardiner, A. H. 'The Coronation of King Ḥaremḥab.' In *J.E.A.* 39 (1953), 13 ff.
11. Goedicke, H. 'Some Remarks on the 400-Year Stela.' In *Chron. d'Ég.* 41 (1966), 23 ff.
12. Hari, R. *Horemheb et la Reine Moutnedjemet, ou la Fin d'une Dynastie*. Geneva, 1965.
13. Harris, J. R. 'How long was the Reign of Ḥoremḥeb?' In *J.E.A.* 54 (1968), 95 ff.
14. Helck, H.-W. 'Das Dekret des Konigs Ḥaremḥab.' In *Z.Ä.S.* 80 (1955), 109 ff.
15. Hölscher, U. and Anthes, R. *The Temples of the Eighteenth Dynasty. The Excavations of Medinet Habu II*. Chicago, 1939.
16. Pflüger, K. *Haremhab und die Amarnazeit. Teildruck: Haremhabs Laufbahn bis zur Thronbesteigung*. Zwickau, 1936.
17. Pflüger, K. 'The Edict of King Haremhab.' In *J.N.E.S.* 5 (1946), 260 ff.
18. Piankoff, A. and Hornung, E. 'Das Grab Amenophis III.' In *Mitt. deutsch. Inst. Kairo*, 17 (1961), 111 ff.
19. Schulman, A. R. 'The Berlin "Trauerrelief" (No. 12411) and some Officials of Tut'ankhamūn and Ay.' In *J.A.R.C.E.* 4 (1965), 55 ff.
20. Seele, K. C. *The Coregency of Ramses II with Seti I and the Date of the Great Hypostyle Hall at Karnak*. Chicago, 1940.
21. Spiegelberg, W. 'Die Datierung des Berliner Trauerreliefs.' In *Z.Ä.S.* 60 (1925), 56 ff.

22. Walle, B. van de and Pflüger, K. 'Le Décret d'Horemheb.' In *Chron. d'Ég.* 22 (1947), 230 ff.
23. Winlock, H. E. 'A Statue of Horemḥab before his Accession.' In *J.E.A.* 10 (1924), 1–5.

VI. THE ROYAL FAMILY AT THE END OF THE EIGHTEENTH DYNASTY

1. Aldred, C. 'The End of the El-'Amārna Period.' In *J.E.A.* 43 (1957), 30 ff.
2. Blankenburg-Van Delden, C. *Large Commemorative Scarabs of Amenophis III*. London, 1969.
3. Gardiner, A. H. 'Tuthmosis III Returns Thanks to Amūn.' In *J.E.A.* 38 (1952), 6 ff.
4. Helck, H.-W. *Der Einfluss der Militärführer in der 18 ägyptischen Dynastie*. Leipzig, 1939.
5. Helck, H.-W. *Zur Verwaltung des mittleren und neuen Reichs*. Leiden–Cologne, 1958.
6. Helck, H.-W. 'Die Tochterheirat ägyptisches Könige.' In *Chron. d'Ég.* 44 (1969), 22 ff.
7. Helck, H.-W. 'Amarna Probleme.' In *Chron. d'Ég.* 44 (1969), 200 ff.
8. Monbrisson, Galerie Simone de: *Arts Antiques*. Paris, n.d.
9. Quibell, J. E. *Tomb of Yuaa and Thuiu (C.C.G. nos. 51001–191)*. Cairo, 1908.
10. Sauneron, S. 'Quelques Monuments de Soumenou au Musée de Brooklyn.' In *Kemi*, 18 (1968), 66 ff.
11. Schiaparelli, E. *Relazione sui lavori della Missione Archeologica Italiana in Egitto, 1903–20*, 1. Turin, n.d.
12. Walle, B. van de. 'La Princesse Isis, fille et épouse d'Amenophis III.' In *Chron. d'Ég.* 43 (1968), 36 ff.
13. Yoyotte, J. 'Le bassin de Djâroukha.' In *Kemi*, 15 (1959), 23 ff.

VII. FOREIGN AFFAIRS

1. Albright, W. F. 'The Egyptian Correspondence of Abimilki, Prince of Tyre.' In *J.E.A.* 23 (1937), 190 ff.
2. Albright, W. F. 'Cuneiform Material for Egyptian Prosopography.' In *J.N.E.S.* 5 (1946), 7 ff.
3. Aldred, C. 'The Foreign Gifts Offered to Pharaoh.' In *J.E.A.* 56 (1970), 105 ff.
4. Kitchen, K. A. *Suppiluliuma and the Amarna Pharaohs: A Study in Relative Chronology*. Liverpool, 1962.
5. Knudtzon, J. A. *et al*. *Die El-Amarna-Tafeln*. 2 vols. Leipzig, 1908, 1915.
6. Langdon, S. and Gardiner, A. H. 'The Treaty of Alliance between Hattušili, King of the Hittites, and the Pharaoh Ramesses II of Egypt.' In *J.E.A.* 6 (1920), 179 ff.
7. Mercer, S. A. B. *The Tell el Amarna Tablets*. 2 vols. Toronto, 1939.
8. Schulman, A. R. 'Some Remarks on the Military Background of the Amarna Period.' In *J.A.R.C.E.* 3 (1964), 51 ff.
9. Winlock, H. E. *The Treasure of Three Egyptian Princesses*. New York, 1948.

VIII. RELIGION, LITERATURE AND ART

1. Aldred, C. 'Hair Styles and History.' In *Bull. M.M.A.* n.s. 15 (1957), 141 ff.
2. Aldred, C. *New Kingdom Art in Ancient Egypt during the Eighteenth Dynasty.* Ed. 2. London, 1961.
3. Aldred, C. 'The "New Year" Gifts to the Pharaoh.' In *J.E.A.* 55 (1969), 73 ff.
4. Anthes, R. *The Head of Queen Nofretete.* Berlin, 1968.
5. Borchardt, L. *Porträts der Königin Nofret-ete aus den Grabungen 1912–13.* In *Tell Amarna.* Leipzig, 1923.
6. Bothmer, B. V. 'Private Sculpture of Dynasty XVIII in Brooklyn.' In *Brooklyn Mus. Annual*, 8 (1966–7), 79–89.
7. Brooklyn Museum: 'Additions to the Museum's Collections: Department of Ancient Art.' In *Brooklyn Mus. Annual*, 10 (1968–9), 167 (No. 69·45).
8. Budge, E. A. W. *Tutānkhamen Amenism, Atenism and Egyptian Monotheism.* London, 1923.
9. Caminos, R. A. *Literary Fragments in the Hieratic Script.* Oxford, 1956.
10. Cooney, J. D. and Simpson, W. K. 'An Architectural Fragment from Amarna.' In *Bull. Brooklyn Mus.* 12, 4 (1951), 1–12.
11. Cooney, J. D. *Amarna Reliefs from Hermopolis in American Collections.* Brooklyn Museum, 1965.
12. Davies, Nina de G. *Ancient Egyptian Paintings.* 3 vols. Chicago, 1936.
13. Desroches-Noblecourt, C. *L'Ancienne Égypte: L'extraordinaire aventure amarnienne.* Paris, 1960.
14. Desroches-Noblecourt, C. *Tutankhamen: Life and death of a pharaoh.* London, 1963.
15. Doresse, M. and J. 'Le Culte d'Aton sous la XVIIIe dynastie avant le schisme amarnien.' In *Jour. Asiatique*, 233 (1941–2), 181 ff.
16. Drioton, É. 'Trois Documents d'Époque Amarnienne.' In *Ann. Serv.* 43 (1944), 15 ff.
17. Erman, A. *The Literature of the Ancient Egyptians, translated from the German by A. M. Blackman.* London, 1927.
18. Erman, A. *Die Religion der Ägypter.* Berlin and Leipzig, 1934.
19. Fecht, G. 'Amarna-Probleme (1–2).' In *Z.Ä.S.* 85 (1960), 83 ff.
20. Fox, P. *Tutankhamun's Treasure.* London, 1951.
21. Frankfort, H. *et al. The Mural Painting of El-ʿAmarneh* (*E.E.S.* 11 F. G. Newton Memorial Volume). London, 1929.
22. Gardiner, A. H. and Nina de G. Davies. *The Tomb of Amenemhet (No. 82).* London, 1915.
23. Gardiner, A. H. 'A Stele in the Macgregor Collection.' In *J.E.A.* 4 (1917), 188 ff.
24. Gardiner, A. H. 'The Astarte Papyrus.' In *Studies Presented to F. Ll. Griffith.* London, 1932. pp. 74 ff.
25. Glanville, S. R. K. 'Some Notes on Material for the Reign of Amenophis III.' In *J.E.A.* 15 (1929), 2 ff.
26. Gunn, B. 'The Religion of the Poor in Ancient Egypt.' In *J.E.A.* 3 (1916), 87 ff.
27. Hassan, S. 'A Representation of the Solar Disk with Human Hands....' In *Ann. Serv.* 38 (1938), 53 ff.
28. Lange, K. and Hirmer, M. *Egypt: Architecture, Sculpture and Painting.* London, 1956.

29. Piankoff, A. 'Les tombeaux de la Vallée des Rois avant et après l'hérésie amarnienne.' In *Bull. soc. fr. égyptol.* Nos. 28–9 (1959), 7 ff.
30. Piankoff, A. 'Les compositions théologiques du nouvel empire égyptien.' In *Bull. Inst. fr. Caire*, 62 (1964), 121 ff.
31. Piankoff, A. 'Les grandes compositions religieuses du nouvel empire et la réforme d'Amarna.' In *Bull. inst. fr. Caire*, 62 (1964), 207 ff.
32. Posener, G. 'La légende égyptienne de la mer insatiable.' In *Annuaire de l'Inst. de philologie et hist. orient. et slaves*, 13 (1953), 461 ff.
33. Posener, G. 'L'exorde de l'instruction éducative d'Amennakhte.' In *Rev. d'Égypt.* 10 (1955), 61 ff.
34. Pritchard, J. B. ed. *Ancient Near Eastern Texts relating to the Old Testament.* Ed. 2. Princeton, 1955.
35. Ranke, H. *Masterpieces of Egyptian Art.* London, 1951.
36. Roeder, G. 'Lebensgrosse Tonmodelle aus einer Altägyptischen Bildhauer Werkstatt.' In *Jahrb. Preuss. Kunstsam.* 62 (1941), 145 ff.
37. Roeder, G. 'Amarna-Blöcke aus Hermopolis.' In *Mitt. deutsch. Inst. Kairo*, 14 (1956), 160 ff.
38. Säve-Söderbergh, T. *Four Eighteenth Dynasty Tombs* (*Private Tombs at Thebes*, 1). Oxford, 1957.
39. Schäfer, H. *Kunstwerke aus El-Amarna* (*Meisterwerke in Berlin*), 2 vols. Berlin, n.d.
40. Schäfer, H. *Amarna in Religion und Kunst.* Leipzig, 1931.
41. Stewart, H. M. 'Traditional Egyptian Sun Hymns of the New Kingdom.' In *Bull. Inst. Archaeol. London*, 6 (1967), 29 ff.
42. Stewart, H. M. 'A Monument with Amarna Traits.' In *Bull. Inst. Archaeol. London*, 7 (1968), 85 ff.
43. Walle, B. van de, *La transmission des textes littéraires égyptiens* (avec une annexe de G. Posener). Brussels, 1948.
44. Williams, C. R. 'Wall Decorations of the Main Temple of the Sun at el-'Amarneh.' In *M.M.A. Studies*, 2 (1930), 135 ff.
45. Witt, C. de. *La Statuaire de Tell el-Amarna.* Antwerp, 1950.
46. Wolf, W. 'Vorläufer der Reformation Echnatons.' In *Z.Ä.S.* 59 (1924), 109 ff.
47. Wolf, W. *Das schöne Fest von Opet; die Festzugdarstellung in grossen Säulengange des Temples von Luksor.* Leipzig, 1931.
48. Wolf, W. *Die Kunst Aegyptens: Gestalt und Geschichte.* Stuttgart, 1957.

Eighteenth Dynasty: 1570–1320 B.C.

Nebpehtyre Amosis	1570–1546 B.C.
Djeserkare Amenophis I	1546–1526 B.C.
Akheperkare Tuthmosis I	1525–c. 1512 B.C.
Akheperenre Tuthmosis II	c. 1512–1504 B.C.
Makare Hatshepsut	1503–1482 B.C.
Menkheperre Tuthmosis III (21)*	1504–1450 B.C.
Akheprure Amenophis II	1450–1425 B.C.
Menkheprure Tuthmosis IV	1425–1417 B.C.
Nebmare Amenophis III	1417–1379 B.C.
Neferkheprure Amenophis IV (Akhenaten)	1379–1362 B.C.
(Ankhkheprure) Smenkhkare (3)*	1364–1361 B.C.
Nebkheprure Tutankhamun	1361–1352 B.C.
Kheperkheprure Ay	1352–1348 B.C.
Djeserkheprure Horemheb	1348–1320 B.C.

* Years of co-regency with his predecessor.